TEACHER'S PET PUBLICATIONS

LITPLAN TEACHER PACK
for
The Good Earth
based on the book by
Pearl Buck

Written by
Mary B. Collins

© 1996 Teacher's Pet Publications
All Rights Reserved

This **LitPlan** for Pearl Buck's
The Good Earth
has been brought to you by Teacher's Pet Publications, Inc.

Copyright Teacher's Pet Publications 1996
11504 Hammock Point
Berlin MD 21811

Only the student materials in this unit plan (such as worksheets, study questions, and tests) may be reproduced multiple times for use in the purchaser's classroom.

For any additional copyright questions,
contact Teacher's Pet Publications.

www.tpet.com

TABLE OF CONTENTS - *The Good Earth*

Introduction	5
Unit Objectives	7
Reading Assignment Sheet	8
Unit Outline	9
Study Questions (Short Answer)	13
Quiz/Study Questions (Multiple Choice)	27
Pre-reading Vocabulary Worksheets	49
Lesson One (Introductory Lesson)	67
Nonfiction Assignment Sheet	68
Oral Reading Evaluation Form	75
Writing Assignment 1	72
Writing Assignment 2	77
Writing Assignment 3	83
Writing Evaluation Form	85
Vocabulary Review Activities	81
Extra Writing Assignments/Discussion ?s	79
Unit Review Activities	88
Unit Tests	91
Unit Resource Materials	125
Vocabulary Resource Materials	139

A FEW NOTES ABOUT THE AUTHOR
Pearl Buck

BUCK, Pearl. (1892-1973). Though American by birth, Pearl S. Buck spent most of her childhood and youth in China. Out of her life and experiences there she wrote many books about the wisdom and patience of the Chinese peasants and about their suffering in war. She won the Nobel prize in 1938.

Pearl Sydenstricker Buck was born on June 26, 1892, in Hillsboro, W. Va. The daughter of Presbyterian missionaries to China, she grew up outside the city of Chinkiang. Pearl attended boarding school in Shanghai and Randolph-Macon Woman's College at Lynchburg, Va. In 1917 she married John Lossing Buck, an American agriculturalist in China. They had one daughter, whose story she told in 'The Child Who Never Grew'.

Buck's first article, "In China, Too," appeared in the Atlantic Monthly in January 1923. Her first book was 'East Wind: West Wind', followed a year later by 'The Good Earth', her most famous novel. Buck wrote more than 85 books. Some of the most successful were 'A House Divided' (1935), 'The Patriot' (1939), and 'Dragon Seed' (1942).

Divorced in 1935, Buck married her publisher, Richard J. Walsh. She established the Pearl S. Buck Foundation of Philadelphia, which has aided in the adoption of Amerasian children. Buck died on March 6, 1973, at her home in Danby, Vt.

-- Courtesy of Compton's Learning Company

INTRODUCTION

This unit has been designed to develop students' reading, writing, thinking, and language skills through exercises and activities related to *The Good Earth* by Pearl Buck. It includes twenty lessons, supported by extra resource materials.

In the **introductory lesson** students are given the materials they will be using during the unit. At the end of the lesson, students begin the pre-reading work for the first reading assignment.

In addition, there is a **nonfiction reading assignment**. Students are required to read two pieces of nonfiction related in some way to *The Good Earth*. After reading their nonfiction pieces, students will fill out a worksheet on which they answer questions regarding facts, interpretation, criticism, and personal opinions. During two class periods, students make **oral presentations** about the nonfiction pieces they have read. This not only exposes all students to a wealth of information, it also gives students the opportunity to practice **public speaking**.

The **reading assignments** are approximately thirty pages each; some are a little shorter while others are a little longer. Students have approximately 15 minutes of pre-reading work to do prior to each reading assignment. This pre-reading work involves reviewing the study questions for the assignment and doing some vocabulary work for 8 to 10 vocabulary words they will encounter in their reading.

The **study guide questions** are fact-based questions; students can find the answers to these questions right in the text. These questions come in two formats: short answer required or multiple choice. The best use of these materials is probably to use the short answer version of the questions as study guides for students (since answers will be more complete), and to use the multiple choice version for occasional quizzes. If your school has the appropriate equipment, it might be a good idea to make transparencies of your answer keys for the overhead projector.

The **vocabulary work** is intended to enrich students' vocabularies as well as to aid in the students' understanding of the book. Prior to each reading assignment, students will complete a two-part worksheet for approximately 8 to 10 vocabulary words in the upcoming reading assignment. Part I focuses on students' use of general knowledge and contextual clues by giving the sentence in which the word appears in the text. Students are then to write down what they think the words mean based on the words' usage. Part II nails down the definitions of the words by giving students dictionary definitions of the words and having students match the words to the correct definitions based on the words' contextual usage. Students should then have an understanding of the words when they meet them in the text.

After each reading assignment, students will go back and formulate answers for the study guide questions. Discussion of these questions serves as a **review** of the most important events and ideas presented in the reading assignments.

After students complete reading the work, there is a **vocabulary review** lesson which pulls together all of the fragmented vocabulary lists for the reading assignments and gives students a review of all of the words they have studied.

A lesson is devoted to the **extra discussion questions/writing assignments**. These questions focus on interpretation, critical analysis and personal response, employing a variety of thinking skills and adding to the students' understanding of the novel.

The **group activity** which follows the discussion questions has students working together to create a film about China using all the information they have gathered through the nonfiction reading assignment, the reading and discussion of the book, and the writing assignments.

There are three **writing assignments** in this unit, each with the purpose of informing, persuading, or having students express personal opinions. The first assignment is **to inform**: in preparation for the oral presentations students make a written composition telling the facts from the nonfiction articles they have read. The second assignment is **to express personal opinions**: students create five questions requiring an opinion for an answer and interview three of their classmates. Following the interviews, students write a composition telling about all the different answers they received in the interviews. The third assignment is **to persuade**: students write the script for a commercial relating to China--a public service commercial, a commercial from a Chinese manufacturer advertising products, or some other commercial the student creates related to China and the material covered in class.

The **review lesson** pulls together all of the aspects of the unit. The teacher is given four or five choices of activities or games to use which all serve the same basic function of reviewing all of the information presented in the unit.

The **unit test** comes in two formats: all multiple choice-matching-true/false or with a mixture of matching, short answer, multiple choice, and composition. As a convenience, two different tests for each format have been included.

There are additional **support materials** included with this unit. The **extra activities section** includes suggestions for an in-class library, crossword and word search puzzles related to the novel, and extra vocabulary worksheets. There is a list of **bulletin board ideas** which gives the teacher suggestions for bulletin boards to go along with this unit. In addition, there is a list of **extra class activities** the teacher could choose from to enhance the unit or as a substitution for an exercise the teacher might feel is inappropriate for his/her class. **Answer keys** are located directly after the **reproducible student materials** throughout the unit. Only the student materials may be reproduced for use in the teacher's classroom without infringement of copyrights.

UNIT OBJECTIVES - *The Good Earth*

1. Through reading Buck's *The Good Earth*, students will better understand the country and people of China.

2. Students will demonstrate their understanding of the text on four levels: factual, interpretive, critical, and personal.

3. Students will consider the traditional values of a rural farming family versus the more modern values of an urban society, and likewise the lifestyle of the poor versus the lifestyle of the rich.

4. Students will consider the cyclical nature of life.

5. Students will be given the opportunity to practice reading aloud and silently to improve their skills in each area.

6. Students will answer questions to demonstrate their knowledge and understanding of the main events and characters in *The Good Earth* as they relate to the author's theme development.

7. Students will enrich their vocabularies and improve their understanding of the novel through the vocabulary lessons prepared for use in conjunction with the novel.

8. The writing assignments in this unit are geared to several purposes:
    a. To have students demonstrate their abilities to inform, to persuade, or to express their own personal ideas
       NOTE: Students will demonstrate ability to write effectively to <u>inform</u> by developing and organizing facts to convey information. Students will demonstrate the ability to write effectively to <u>persuade</u> by selecting and organizing relevant information, establishing an argumentative purpose, and by designing an appropriate strategy for an identified audience. Students will demonstrate the ability to write effectively to <u>express personal ideas</u> by selecting a form and its appropriate elements.
    b. To check the students' reading comprehension
    c. To make students think about the ideas presented by the novel
    d. To encourage logical thinking
    e. To provide an opportunity to practice good grammar and improve students' use of the English language.

9. Students will read aloud, report, and participate in large and small group discussions to improve their public speaking and personal interaction skills.

READING ASSIGNMENT SHEET - *The Good Earth*

Date Assigned	Chapters Assigned	Completion Date
	1-5	
	6-7	
	8-10	
	11-14	
	15-17	
	18-21	
	22-29	
	30-34	

UNIT OUTLINE - *The Good Earth*

1 Introduction PVR 1-4	2 Study ?s 1-4 Library	3 Writing Assignment #1 PVR 5-9	4 Study ?s 5-9 Reports PVR 10-14	5 Reports
6 Study ?s 10-14 Reports PVR 15-19	7 Study ?s 15-19 PVR 20-23	8 Study ?s 20-23 Writing Assignment #2 PVR 24-27	9 Study ?s 24-27 PVR 28-30	10 Study?s 28-30 PVR 31-34
11 Study?s 31-34 Extra ?s	12 Vocabulary	13 Writing Assignment #3	14 Project	15 Project
16 Project	17 Filming	18 View Film	19 Review	20 Test

Key: P=Preview Study Questions V=Prereading Vocabulary Worksheet R=Read

STUDY GUIDE QUESTIONS

SHORT ANSWER STUDY GUIDE QUESTIONS - *The Good Earth*

Chapters 1 - 4
1. Who is Wang Lung?
2. What do we learn about Wang Lung as we see him making preparations for his wedding day?
3. Describe Wang Lung's entrance into the House of Hwang on his wedding day.
4. Who is O-lan? Describe her.
5. What big news did O-lan casually mention to Wang Lung in the field?
6. Under what conditions would O-lan reappear at the House of Hwang?
7. Why did Wang Lung say that O-lan was "a woman such as is not commonly found"?
8. What did Wang Lung do to celebrate the birth of his first son?
9. Why did Wang Lung walk "among his fellows . . . at ease with himself and all"?

Chapters 5 - 9
1. Why were the cakes and the visit to the House of Hwang important?
2. Why did Wang Lung and O-lan loudly claim that their child was a female with smallpox and pray for its death?
3. Why did Wang Lung buy the Hwang's land?
4. Of what had Wang Lung's Hwang parcel of land become a symbol?
5. What was Wang Lung's reaction to O-lan's announcement of her second pregnancy? Why?
6. How was the delivery and acceptance of the second boy different from the first?
7. Why did Wang Lung's uncle and uncle's wife have an "evil destiny"?
8. Why did Wang Lung give money to his uncle?
9. What made Wang Lung sad?
10. "He would, he told himself, in spite of gods and drought, do that which he had determined." What did Wang Lung do?
11. Why did O-lan kill the ox?
12. Who was responsible for the raid on Wang Lung's house?
13. Why did Wang Lung's purchase of land turn out to be a good thing?
14. How did Wang Lung show his anger to the gods?
15. Why did Wang Lung want to go south?
16. How did Wang Lung's new-born child die? Why?
17. Again, Wang Lung's uncle is shown to be a shady character. What two new pieces of evidence for this are we given in Chapter 9?
18. How did Wang Lung and O-lan get the money to go south?

Good Earth Short Answer Study Questions Page 2

Chapters 10 - 14
1. How did they travel south even though they were so weak?
2. Who helped Wang Lung know what to do in the city?
3. Why did Wang Lung's father not beg?
4. How did Pearl Buck aptly describe Wang Lung's life in the city?
5. What did Wang Lung learn from taking the American woman as a fare?
6. Why would Wang Lung not eat the meat?
7. Selling a female child into slavery was a commonly accepted means of survival for the poor. Why didn't Wang Lung sell his baby girl?
8. What was "over the wall"?
9. How was Wang Lung different from the other poor men around him?
10. What difference between Wang Lung and the crowd does Wang Lung's innocent question, "Sir, is there any way whereby the rich who oppress us can make it rain so that I can work on the land" show us?
11. Why were soldiers arresting the poor men?
12. How did Wang Lung escape the soldiers?
13. What gave Wang Lung the idea of taking money?
14. Why did Wang Lung take the money?

Chapters 15-19
1. What did Wang Lung buy with his money?
2. Who ruined Wang Lung's house while he was away?
3. What did O-lan have hidden in cloth?
4. With whom did Wang Lung strike a bargain for Hwang's land? Why?
5. What changes did Wang Lung make after purchasing the Hwang land?
6. What was wrong with Wang Lung's eldest girl?
7. Why did Wang Lung send his sons to school?
8. What change occurred in Wang Lung in the seventh year of his prosperity?
9. What gave Wang Lung the courage to ask for Lotus?
10. What sickness did Wang Lung get?
11. What did O-lan say when Wang Lung came home without his braid?

Good Earth Short Answer Study Questions Page 3

Chapters 20 - 23
 1. Who negotiated the bringing of Lotus into Wang Lung's house?
 2. Why did Wang Lung leave O-lan alone?
 3. What was O-lan's reaction to Lotus?
 4. Why was there trouble between O-lan and Cuckoo?
 5. Why didn't Wang Lung want Lotus to be friends with his uncle's wife?
 6. What finally made Wang Lung angry with Lotus?
 7. What healed Wang Lung's sickness?
 8. Why did Wang Lung keep Lotus after he no longer had a sickness for her?
 9. What explanation did O-lan give for the eldest son's behavior?
10. How did Wang Lung propose to control his son?
11. For what advice did Wang Lung go to Lotus?
12. Who arranged the marriage of the eldest son? Why?
13. Why did Wang Lung go to see Yang?
14. Why did Wang Lung want his uncle, nephew and uncle's wife out of the house?
15. Why did Wang Lung allow his uncle's family to stay?

Chapters 24 - 27
1. Why did Wang Lung send his eldest son away to school?
2. On what business did Wang Lung go to see the merchant?
3. What was his daughter's reply when Wang Lung asked her why she wept?
4. After his children were betrothed, how did Wang Lung's opinion (view) of O-lan change?
5. What was the doctor's verdict?
6. What were O-lan's final words to Cuckoo?
7. What were O-lan's wishes? Were they carried out?
8. By what means did Wang Lung and his son decide to make the uncle's family less of a nuisance?
9. Why did Wang Lung send his daughter to the home of her future husband?

Good Earth Short Answer Study Questions Page 4

Chapters 28 - 30
1. What effect did the great flood have on Wang Lung's fortunes?
2. Why did the eldest son suggest moving to the Hwang home?
3. What kind of a wife did Wang Lung's second son want?
4. Where did Wang Lung's nephew go?
5. Who moved first to the House of Hwang?
6. When did the rest of the family move to the Hwang house?
7. Why did the eldest son want to decorate the house so well?
8. What was the second son's reaction to the eldest son's spending?
9. What promise did Wang Lung make to his uncle's wife?

Chapters 31 - 34
1. Who came to stay at Wang Lung's Hwang house?
2. What problem did the nephew cause at the Hwang house?
3. What did the nephew leave behind?
4. What promise did Wang Lung make and keep to the nephew's slave woman?
5. Where did Wang Lung's third son want to go?
6. How did Wang Lung try to satisfy the third son?
7. How did Wang Lung satisfy Lotus when he took Pear Blossom?
8. How did each of Wang Lung's sons react to Wang Lung's having Pear Blossom?
9. Why did the third son leave?
10. What promise did Pear Blossom make to Wang Lung?
11. Where did Wang Lung go to die and who went with him?
12. What would the two remaining sons do after Wang Lung died?

ANSWER KEY: SHORT ANSWER STUDY GUIDE QUESTIONS - *The Good Earth*

Chapters 1 - 4

1. Who is Wang Lung?
    He is a young farmer who lives alone with his father and cares for him and the farm.

2. What do we learn about Wang Lung as we see him making preparations for his wedding day?
    Although he is poor and recognizes his social status, he has pride. He is not well educated in the ways of the world. He is an honest, good-hearted young man whose "religion" is mixed with superstition.

3. Describe Wang Lung's entrance into the House of Hwang on his wedding day.
    He approaches the great house with fear and apprehension; mostly because he is of such a lower social standing, but also because he is coming for his wife and isn't sure what to do or to expect. The gateman takes advantage of Wang Lung's innocence and treats him roughly.

4. Who is O-lan? Describe her.
    She is Wang Lung's new wife. She is not pretty, being tall and broad-featured with large feet. She is calm, quiet, hard-working, eager to please, and possesses a great deal of inner strength.

5. What big news did O-lan casually mention to Wang Lung in the field?
    She mentioned that she was pregnant.

6. Under what conditions would O-lan reappear at the House of Hwang?
    "When I return to that house it will be with my son in my arms. I shall have a red coat on him and red-flowered trousers and on his head a hat with a small gilded Buddha sen on the front and on his feet tiger-faced shoes. And I will wear new shoes and a new coat of black sateen and I will go into the kitchen where I spent my days and I will go into the great hall where the Old One sits with her opium, and I will show myself and my son to all of them."

7. Why did Wang Lung say that O-lan was "a woman such as is not commonly found"?
    O-lan worked side-by-side with him in the fields until it was time for the baby to come. While in labor, she prepared the evening meal, then she went alone to her room to have the baby. All she required from Wang Lung was for him to give her a sharp reed with which to cut the cord. Then, after giving birth, she cleaned the baby, herself and her room.

8. What did Wang Lung do to celebrate the birth of his first son?
   He bought eggs to die red and give to his friends and neighbors for good luck, and he burned incense for the gods.

9. Why did Wang Lung walk "among his fellows . . . at ease with himself and all"?
   He had a good wife, a healthy son, plenty to eat and money saved away.

Chapters 5 - 9
1. Why were the cakes and the visit to the House of Hwang important?
   The cakes and the son's attire were an outward sign to the Hwang family of Wang Lung's prosperity. He could return to the House of Hwang as a little more than a very poor farmer, and in this he took pride.

2. Why did Wang Lung and O-lan loudly claim that their child was a female with smallpox and pray for its death?
   They had been rejoicing in their good fortune (and the Hwang family's misfortune). They were afraid the gods would strike against them for being so happy. It was their attempt to fool the gods.

3. Why did Wang Lung buy the Hwang's land?
   He had money to do so, it was good land which had been owned by a well-respected family, and he had a great personal attachment to the value of land.

4. Of what had Wang Lung's Hwang parcel of land become a symbol?
   It had become a sign and a symbol of his determination to buy enough land to make that first parcel seem insignificant in size.

5. What was Wang Lung's reaction to O-lan's announcement of her second pregnancy? Why?
   He was cross with her, complaining that she wouldn't be able to work during the harvest. He was over-tired; working so much land was a strain on him and made him irritable.

6. How was the delivery and acceptance of the second boy different from the first?
   Again O-lan worked in the field until just before the birth of the child. This time, however, Wang Lung didn't even go into the house with her to see if it was a boy or a girl. After the delivery, O-lan came back to work with him in the field before sunset. After the work, dinner and washing, Wang Lung finally looked at the child.

7. Why did Wang Lung's uncle and uncle's wife have an "evil destiny"?
   They were lazy, shiftless people who brought about most of their misfortunes themselves.

8. Why did Wang Lung give money to his uncle?
    After he refused his uncle, saying he worked hard for his money (and implied that his uncle was idle), the uncle threatened to tell the townspeople of Wang Lung's disrespect. Since Wang Lung had pride in his reputation, he finally agreed to give his uncle the money to keep him quiet.

9. What made Wang Lung sad?
    A sense of evil and misfortune had come to his house. His uncle had taken his money, a girl was born, and it would be at least another year before he could buy more land.

10. "He would, he told himself, in spite of gods and drought, do that which he had determined." What did Wang Lung do?
    He bought more land from the Hwangs.

11. Why did O-lan kill the ox?
    They had no food for themselves or the ox, so O-lan killed the ox for food. O-lan killed the ox because Wang Lung couldn't bear to kill his friend and working partner.

12. Who was responsible for the raid on Wang Lung's house?
    Wang Lung's uncle had told people that Wang Lung had food and money stored away, so the starving people came to steal his goods.

13. Why did Wang Lung's purchase of land turn out to be a good thing?
    If he had money or food, it would have been stolen. The robbers could not take his land.

14. How did Wang Lung show his anger to the gods?
    He shouted that they were wicked and went out and spat upon their images at the temple.

15. Why did Wang Lung want to go south?
    He wanted to try to find food and work. He thought it better than sitting on the farm and dying.

16. How did Wang Lung's new-born child die? Why?
    O-lan choked it to death. They had nothing to feed it; it would have died of starvation.

17. Again, Wang Lung's uncle is shown to be a shady character. What two new pieces of evidence for this are we given in Chapter 9?
    He has eaten and brings men to buy land from Wang Lung at cheap prices.

18. How did Wang Lung and O-lan get the money to go south?
    They sold their furniture.

Chapters 10 - 14

1. How did they travel south even though they were so weak?
    They took the train.

2. Who helped Wang Lung know what to do in the city?
    A man on the train helped him.

3. Why did Wang Lung's father not beg?
    He was an old man who felt he had done his work in his day and that his son and son's family should provide for him in his old age.

4. How did Pearl Buck aptly describe Wang Lung's life in the city?
    "He lived in the rich city as alien as a rat in a rich man's house that is fed on scraps thrown away, and hides here and there and is never a part of the real life of the house."

5. What did Wang Lung learn from taking the American woman as a fare?
    "Nevertheless, through this experience Wang Lung had learned what the young men had not taught him, that he belonged to his own kind, who have black hair and black eyes . . . ."

6. Why would Wang Lung not eat the meat?
    His second son stole the meat. Having a sense of pride and morality, Wang Lung would not have any part of this wrong thing his son did.

7. Selling a female child into slavery was a commonly accepted means of survival for the poor. Why didn't Wang Lung sell his baby girl?
    He didn't have the heart to sell her. He loved her and couldn't think of her in slavery; it seemed immoral.

8. What was "over the wall"?
    A rich man's home filled with jewels, food, and riches beyond belief was beyond the wall.

9. How was Wang Lung different from the other poor men around him?
    Wang Lung had land and knew the value of land. He also had a great deal of personal pride.

10. What difference between Wang Lung and the crowd does Wang Lung's innocent question, "Sir, is there any way whereby the rich who oppress us can make it rain so that I can work on the land" show us?
    The crowd wants the rich to share with the poor; it implies the crowd (poor) shall have things without hard labor. Wang Lung doesn't want charity; he wants only to be able to work his land to make a life for his family.

11. Why were soldiers arresting the poor men?
    They were arresting them to recruit them to carry goods and run errands -- to be soldiers.

12. How did Wang Lung escape the soldiers?
    He hid in the hut by day and came out only at night after the soldiers were gone.

13. What gave Wang Lung the idea of taking money?
    The man Wang Lung found on the inside of the wall offered him money if he would spare his life.

14. Why did Wang Lung take the money?
    He saw it as his only way to get back to his land without selling his girl.

Chapters 15-19
1. What did Wang Lung buy with his money?
    He bought things to fix the farm and house and a few extras.

2. Who ruined Wang Lung's house while he was away?
    His uncle and his uncle's band of robbers ruined it.

3. What did O-lan have hidden in cloth?
    She had a packet of jewels she had taken from the rich man's house in the south.

4. With whom did Wang Lung strike a bargain for Hwang's land? Why?
    He bargained with an old servant woman named Cuckoo. She was the only one left to be the go-between for the lord.

5. What changes did Wang Lung make after purchasing the Hwang land?
    He built an addition onto his house, bought a donkey, bought Ching's farm and hired Ching to help with his lands, set his children to work in the fields, and did not permit O-lan to work in the fields. Later he built a new house and hired more workers.

6. What was wrong with Wang Lung's eldest girl?
    She was retarded, presumably because of being starved as a baby.

7. Why did Wang Lung send his sons to school?
    It was a shame to him that no one in his family could read or write. He also needed someone to protect his interests at the market.

8. What change occurred in Wang Lung in the seventh year of his prosperity?
    He saw O-lan as ugly and he lost his feelings for her. He became bored and restless at home.

9. What gave Wang Lung the courage to ask for Lotus?
    Cuckoo, now working at the tea house, said, "Ah, it is only the farmer!" which angered Wang Lung and made him want to show her that he was as good as other men who came to the tea house for pleasure.

10. What sickness did Wang Lung get?
    He was love-sick, infatuated with Lotus. He forgot all his business but his time with her.

11. What did O-lan say when Wang Lung came home without his braid?
    "You have cut off your life!"

Chapters 20 - 23
1. Who negotiated the bringing of Lotus into Wang Lung's house?
    Cuckoo and Wang Lung's uncle's wife did the negotiating.

2. Why did Wang Lung leave O-lan alone?
    He was ashamed before her.

3. What was O-lan's reaction to Lotus?
    She avoided her. On the day of her arrival, O-lan took the children and went to the fields.

4. Why was there trouble between O-lan and Cuckoo?
    Cuckoo had been a servant in the Hwang house at the same time as O-lan. Cuckoo had been mean with O-lan, and their hatred grew from those old days. Wang Lung built a separate kitchen and room for Cuckoo to help bring peace to his house.

5. Why didn't Wang Lung want Lotus to be friends with his uncle's wife?
    He didn't like his uncle's wife; she was a shady character. He wanted Lotus to remain as pure as he thought she was.

6. What finally made Wang Lung angry with Lotus?
    She called his children idiots and filthy children, at which he took great offense.

7. What healed Wang Lung's sickness?
    Working the land healed him.

8. Why did Wang Lung keep Lotus after he no longer had a sickness for her?
    He kept her partly as a toy to be used when he felt like it, and partly to show the villagers he could afford to keep a non-working person in his home for his pleasure.

9. What explanation did O-lan give for the eldest son's behavior?
    "You [Wang Lung] worked on the land. But he is like a young lord and he is idle in the house."

10. How did Wang Lung propose to control his son?
    He wanted to find him a wife and marry him off.

11. For what advice did Wang Lung go to Lotus?
    He wanted to see if she knew of anyone who would make a good wife for his eldest son.

12. Who arranged the marriage of the eldest son? Why?
    Cuckoo made the arrangements because she knew the merchant whose daughter was intended to be the bride.

13. Why did Wang Lung go to see Yang?
    He wanted to pay her off to refuse his son and send him home.

14. Why did Wang Lung want his uncle, nephew and uncle's wife out of the house?
    They were a bad influence on his son; his nephew had lured his son to a prostitute.

15. Why did Wang Lung allow his uncle's family to stay?
    He discovered that his uncle was an official in a band of robbers. He was afraid that the robbers would destroy his home and harm his family, so he let his uncle stay.

Chapters 24 - 27

1. Why did Wang Lung send his eldest son away to school?
    He had time to kill before the marriage would take place, and he found his son with Lotus.

2. On what business did Wang Lung go to see the merchant?
    He went to ask him to take his second son as an apprentice. He also asked if the merchant had a son for his second daughter.

3. What was his daughter's reply when Wang Lung asked her why she wept?
    She said she cried because her mother bound her feet, but Wang Lung had never heard her cry because "my mother said I was not to weep aloud because you are too kind and weak for pain and you might say to leave me as I am, and then my husband would not love me, even as you do not love her."

4. After his children were betrothed, how did Wang Lung's opinion (view) of O-lan change?
    He felt sorry that he had grown away from her, but he consoled himself with the fact that he had not beaten her and had treated her fairly in the eyes of the laws and customs.

5. What was the doctor's verdict?
    O-lan would die.

6. What were O-lan's final words to Cuckoo?
   "Well, and you may have lived in the courts of the Old Lord, and you were accounted beautiful, but I have been a man's wife and I have borne him sons, and you are still a slave."

7. What were O-lan's wishes? Were they carried out?
   She wished that Cuckoo and Lotus would not be allowed in her room or to touch her things when she is gone, and she wished to see her son wed before she died. Yes, these wishes were granted.

8. By what means did Wang Lung and his son decide to make the uncle's family less of a nuisance?
   They decided to give the uncle's family opium.

9. Why did Wang Lung send his daughter to the home of her future husband?
   He sent her to protect her from his uncle's son.

Chapters 28 - 30

1. What effect did the great flood have on Wang Lung's fortunes?
   He gained by it. People bought up his grain at high prices. He bought their land when they wanted to sell it, and he lent them money to start their farms again after the flood was over. It increased his social position considerably.

2. Why did the eldest son suggest moving to the Hwang home?
   He wanted to get away from his cousin, to get closer to town where things were going on, and to get a better house for people to admire.

3. What kind of a wife did Wang Lung's second son want?
   "I desire a maid from a village, of good landed family and without poor relatives, and one who will bring a good dowry with her, neither plain nor fair to look upon, and a good cook, so that even though there are servants in the kitchen she may watch them. And she must be such a one that if she buys cloth the garment will be well cut so that the scraps of cloth left over should lie in the palm of her hand."

4. Where did Wang Lung's nephew go?
   He went off to join the war, to see different parts of the country.

5. Who moved first to the House of Hwang?
   Cuckoo and Lotus, and the eldest son with his wife and servants moved into the House of Hwang first.

6. When did the rest of the family move to the Hwang house?
   The rest of the family moved in after Ching died.

7. Why did the eldest son want to decorate the house so well?
   He wanted the people who would come to the wedding to be impressed.

8. What was the second son's reaction to the eldest son's spending?
   He didn't like it. He was very thrifty.

9. What promise did Wang Lung make to his uncle's wife?
   He promised that if her son would return, he would find a wife for him.

Chapters 31 - 34
1. Who came to stay at Wang Lung's Hwang house?
   His nephew and some soldiers came.

2. What problem did the nephew cause at the Hwang house?
   He was chasing the women. He wanted Lotus' servant girl, but the girl begged Wang Lung to find another, and another did volunteer.

3. What did the nephew leave behind?
   He left behind a child to the servant girl.

4. What promise did Wang Lung make and keep to the nephew's slave woman?
   He promised to find her a husband and father for her daughter.

5. Where did Wang Lung's third son want to go?
   He wanted to go off to the wars.

6. How did Wang Lung try to satisfy the third son?
   He suggested school or marriage or that the boy would have a slave. The son suggested he wanted Pear Blossom, Lotus' slave. Wang Lung denies him.

7. How did Wang Lung satisfy Lotus when he took Pear Blossom?
   He gave her the material things she wanted.

8. How did each of Wang Lung's sons react to Wang Lung's having Pear Blossom?
   The eldest son said, "You may do as you like." The second son said nothing. The third son left and went to be a soldier.

9. Why did the third son leave?
   His father was a hypocrite. He wouldn't allow the son to take Pear Blossom, but he took her for himself. This was the final thing in a whole list of things with which the third son disagreed.

10. What promise did Pear Blossom make to Wang Lung?
    She promised to take care of Wang Lung's eldest girl, "the fool," after his death.

11. Where did Wang Lung go to die and who went with him?
    He went back to his house on the land with Pear Blossom, his eldest girl and some servants.

12. What would the two remaining sons do after Wang Lung died?
    They would sell his land and divide the profits.

MULTIPLE CHOICE STUDY GUIDE/QUIZ QUESTIONS - *The Good Earth*

Chapters 1-4

1. Who is Wang Lung?
    a. He is the owner of a large estate.
    b. He is a young farmer.
    c. He is a poor merchant.
    d. He is a soldier.

2. We learn many things about Wang Lung as we see him making preparations for his wedding day. Which is not one of them?
    a. He has a good education for his class.
    b. He is poor and recognizes his social status, but he has pride.
    c. He is honest and good-hearted.
    d. His "religion" is mixed with superstition.

3. Describe Wang Lung's entrance into the House of Hwang on his wedding day.
    a. He is calm and confident, and is treated with respect by the gateman.
    b. He approaches with fear and apprehension, and the gateman treats him roughly.
    c. He enters acting as if he is already the master of the house, which was the custom.
    d. He attempts to enter, but he is turned away at the gate.

4. Which of the following does not describe O-Lan?
    a. She is very pretty.
    b. She is tall.
    c. She is calm and quiet.
    d. She possesses a great deal of inner strength.

5. What big news did O-Lan casually mention to Wang Lung in the field?
    a. She has inherited a fortune from a dead uncle.
    b. She was married before she married Wang Lung.
    c. She is terminally sick.
    d. She is pregnant.

Good Earth Multiple Choice Study/Quiz Questions Page 2

6. O-lan gives the following description to Wang Lung: "When I return . . . . it will be with my son in my arms. I shall have a red coat on him and red-flowered trousers and on his head a hat with a small gilded Buddha sewn on the front and on his feet tiger-faced shoes. And I will wear new shoes and a new coat of black sateen and I will . . . show myself and my son to all of them." Where does she speak of going?
    a. She speaks of returning to see her family.
    b. She talks about going to the great temple in the city.
    c. She speaks of her return to the House of Hwang.
    d. She is talking about going into town on her first day out as a new mother.

7. Why did Wang-Lung say that O-lan was "a woman such as is not commonly found"?
    a. She could read and write, although she rarely told people that she could.
    b. She did all of her usual jobs until it was time to deliver the baby. After the birth, she cleaned everything up herself.
    c. He was amazed that she got pregnant as quickly as she did, and made sure she had a son for her first born.
    d. She could do as much work as a man and still be a pretty and loving wife.

8. What did Wang Lung do to celebrate the birth of his first son?
    a. He gave his friends eggs that had been dyed red, and burned incense for the gods.
    b. He donated a large amount of money to the temple to thank the gods for such a blessing.
    c. He set off firecrackers and bought candy for all the children in the town.
    d. He celebrated and got drunk.

9. Wang Lung walked "among his fellows . . . at ease with himself and all" because he had a good wife, a healthy son, plenty to eat, and money saved away.
    a. True
    b. False

Good Earth Multiple Choice Study/Quiz Questions Page 3

Chapters 5-9

10. Why were the cakes and the visit to the house of Hwang important?
    a. The cakes and the son's attire were an outward sign to the Hwang family of Wang Lung's prosperity.
    b. In the superstitious religion of the simple farmers, they insured the newborn's place in the hereafter.
    c. Since they were the richest family in the area, they could demand that any child they wanted be brought to them. This was Wang Lung's way of showing that he could give them money in return for the privilege of keeping his child.
    d. He was very superstitious. He thought that showing respect to the rich family would bring good fortune on his son.

11. Wang Lung and O-lan had been rejoicing in their good fortune (and the Hwang family's misfortune). Then they loudly claimed that their child was a female with smallpox, and prayed for its death because they were afraid the gods would strike against them for being so happy. It was their attempt to fool the gods.
    a. True
    b. False

12. Which of the following is not one of the reasons Wang Lung bought the Hwang's land?
    a. He had money to do so.
    b. He thought some of the Hwang ancestors had hidden their treasures on the land. He wanted to dig and try to find it.
    c. It had been owned by a well-respected family.
    d. He had a great personal attachment to the value of land.

13. Wang Lung's purchase of the Hwang parcel of land became symbolic of his growing greed and materialism.
    a. True
    b. False

14. Wang Lung was cross when O-lan announced her second pregnancy. He complained that she wouldn't be able to work during the harvest.
    a. True
    b. False

15. Which of the following things happened after the birth of the second child?
    a. Wang Lung stopped work and went in to see it.
    b. O-lan went back to work in the field.
    c. Grandfather held the baby while O-lan rested.
    d. O-lan took the baby to the field to show Wang Lung.

Good Earth Multiple Choice Study/Quiz Questions Page 4

16. Why did Wang Lung's uncle and uncle's wife have an "evil destiny"?
    a. His uncle was the third child born in the third month of the third day. This was considered to be very unlucky.
    b. They were lazy and shiftless, and brought most of their misfortunes on themselves.
    c. His uncle's wife had been injured as a young woman, and was not well. She was considered a jinx on the rest of the family.
    d. His uncle did not believe in the power of the gods. The religious people of the village thought this was the cause of his problems.

17. Why did Wang Lung give money to his uncle?
    a. He had promised his father he would do so.
    b. He was afraid of what the gods would do to him and his family if he refused.
    c. O-lan made him do it. She felt sorry for them. He did it to please her.
    d. His uncle threatened to tell the townspeople that Wang Lung was disrespectful. Since Wang Lung had pride in his reputation, he gave in.

18. Several things made Wang Lung sad. Which was not one of them?
    a. A sense of evil and misfortune had come to his house.
    b. He was having a lot of physical problems.
    c. A girl was born.
    d. It would be another year before they could buy more land.

19. "He would," he told himself, "in spite of the gods and drought, do that which he had determined." What did Wang Lung do?
    a. He bought more land from the Hwangs.
    b. He raised two crops in one year.
    c. He bought new clothes and furniture.
    d. He harvested his entire crop by himself.

20. Why did O-lan kill the ox?
    a. It was a sacrifice to appease the angry gods.
    b. She was angry at Wang Lung, and it was the only way to get his attention.
    c. They needed it for food, and Wang Lung could not bear to do the deed.
    d. It was diseased and she was afraid it would infect the children.

21. Who was responsible for the raid on Wang Lung's house?
    a. It was the Red Army.
    b. It was the eldest son of the House of Hwang.
    c. It was the priest from the temple.
    d. It was Wang Lung's uncle.

Good Earth Multiple Choice Study/Quiz Questions Page 5

22. Was Wang Lung's purchase of land a good or bad thing?
    a. It was bad because he had used all of his money for land, but he couldn't afford to feed his family or buy seed to plant.
    b. It was good because if he had had food or money it would have been stolen.
    c. It was bad because it angered the Hwangs.
    d. It was good because it appeased the gods; it showed them that Wang Lung was still connected to the land, which symbolically meant he had good, basic values.

23. How did Wang Lung show his anger to the gods?
    a. He broke their statues.
    b. He shook his fist at the sky and cursed.
    c. He dressed in white, the color of mourning, for five days.
    d. He shouted that they were wicked and went and spat on their images at the temple.

24. What did Wang Lung do to try and find food and work?
    a. He asked for work at the temple but was turned away.
    b. He went south.
    c. He went out at night, looking for scraps in people's trash.
    d. He offered a sacrifice to the gods and begged for help.

25. What happened at the birth of Wang Lung's child?
    a. It was born dead.
    b. O-lan asked another woman to nurse the child, since she could not.
    c. O-lan choked it to death.
    d. The family celebrated, even though they had little else to be happy about.

26. Again, Wang Lung's uncle is shown to be a shady character. What two new pieces of evidence for this are we given in Chapter 9?
    a. He is wearing jewelry and new clothes.
    b. He has a new servant girl and two sacks of rice.
    c. He tries to talk Wang Lung into leaving his father outside to die and giving the extra food to his (the uncle's) family.
    d. He has eaten and brings men to buy Wang Lung's land at a cheap price.

27. How did Wang Lung and O-lan get the money to go south?
    a. They sold their furniture.
    b. They sold some land.
    c. They had money hidden in a hole under the house, and they used it.
    d. They borrowed it from the uncle at an extremely high rate of interest.

Good Earth Multiple Choice Study/Quiz Questions Page 6

Chapters 10-14

28. How did they travel south even though they were so weak?
    a. They stole a donkey and took turns riding it.
    b. They went by train.
    c. They traveled a little bit at a time and took a lot of rest breaks.
    d. They went by boat.

29. Who helped Wang Lung know what to do in the city?
    a. A man from the University was helping all of the refugees.
    b. His brother lived in the city and helped him.
    c. A man from the train helped him.
    d. No one helped him. He watched what was going on and learned by himself.

30. Did Wang Lung's father beg?
    a. Yes, he felt it was his duty as head of the household to set the example for the rest of the family.
    b. No, he felt that he had already done his work and that his son should provide for him.
    c. Yes, he felt that one is never too old to pitch in and help; it is an honor to be of service.
    d. No, he would rather die of starvation than be so humiliated.

31. How did Pearl Buck aptly describe Wang Lung's life in the city?
    a. ". . . as a rat in a rich man's house"
    b. ". . . as a fish out of water"
    c. ". . . as a fly in honey"
    d. ". . . as a maggot on the good earth"

32. What did Wang Lung learn from taking the American woman as a fare?
    a. He learned not to trust foreigners.
    b. He learned his way around the city.
    c. He learned that he belonged to his own kind.
    d. He learned patience.

33. Why would Wang Lung not eat the meat?
    a. He was a strict vegetarian for religious reasons. Even starvation could not tempt him to go against his beliefs.
    b. He wanted to save it for his family.
    c. He was too tired to eat anything.
    d. His son had stolen the meat, and Wang Lung would have nothing to do with it.

Good Earth Multiple Choice Study/Quiz Questions Page 7

34. Selling a female child into slavery was a commonly accepted means of survival for the poor. Did Wang Lung sell his baby girl?
    a. Yes, he did so gladly to get rid of the bad luck.
    b. No, he could not part with her.
    c. Yes, he did so, but with great hesitation.
    d. No, he couldn't get enough money for her to make it worthwhile.

35. What was "over the wall"?
    a. It was a large monastery where the monks were giving out food.
    b. It was a herd of cattle.
    c. It was the home and fortune of a very rich man.
    d. It was a large garden full of ripe fruits and vegetables.

36. How was Wang Lung different from the other poor men around him?
    a. He had land and knew the value of it.
    b. He had brought his family with him.
    c. He was the only man from the north, and still had his braid of hair.
    d. He was the only one who spoke his dialect.

37. Wang Lung agreed with the crowd. He wanted to have the riches without hard labor.
    a. True
    b. False

38. What were the soldiers doing?
    a. They were killing the women and children.
    b. They were taking money and food from all of the people.
    c. They were arresting the men and recruiting them to be soldiers.
    d. They were shooting everyone in their path.

39. How did Wang Lung escape the soldiers?
    a. He dressed like a woman.
    b. He left the city for a week and hid in the country.
    c. He hid by the hut by day and came out at night after the soldiers were gone.
    d. He pretended to be lame and dumb. They didn't want him.

40. How did Wang Lung get the money?
    a. He found it in the safe in the house.
    b. The man offered it to him in return for his life.
    c. He took it from one of the other beggars.
    d. He found it by accident -- it was lying in a sack on the ground.

Good Earth Multiple Choice Study/Quiz Questions Page 8

41. Did Wang Lung take the money?
    a. Yes, he saw it as the only way to get back to his land without selling his daughter.
    b. Yes, he figured he might as well have it as someone else.
    c. No, his pride and moral convictions would not let him take it.
    d. No, someone else stole it from him.

Good Earth Multiple Choice Study/Quiz Questions Page 9

Chapters 15-19

42. What did Wang Lung do with his money?
    a. He bought train tickets back home.
    b. He bought food for his family and they had a feast.
    c. He bought things to fix the farm and house and a few extras.
    d. He hid it in a hole under the house.

43. What happened to Wang Lung's house while he was away?
    a. Nothing happened. His friend and neighbor took care of it.
    b. It was destroyed by a great wind.
    c. His uncle and his uncle's band of robbers ruined it.
    d. It caught fire and burned to the ground.

44. What did O-lan have hidden in the cloth?
    a. She had a bag of seeds to start a new crop.
    b. She had a knife.
    c. She had a few crusts of bread. She was so used to being hungry that she still saved every morsel of food.
    d. She had a packet of jewels she had taken from the rich man's house.

45. With whom did Wang Lung strike a bargain for Hwang's land?
    a. He talked to Hwang himself.
    b. He talked to an old servant woman named Cuckoo.
    c. He talked to the gate-keeper who had ridiculed him when he had come so many years earlier for O-lan.
    d. He talked to the eldest son.

46. Wang Lung made several changes after purchasing the Hwang land. Which of the following was not one of the changes?
    a. He painted his house red, the color of prosperity.
    b. He bought a donkey.
    c. He hired Ching to help him.
    d. He set his children to work in the fields.

47. What was wrong with Wang Lung's eldest girl?
    a. She was blind.
    b. She could not walk.
    c. She was retarded.
    d. She was deaf.

Good Earth Multiple Choice Study/Quiz Questions Page 10

48. What did Wang Lung do about his sons?
    a. He sent them to work in the fields so they could appreciate all he had done for them.
    b. He sent them to school to learn to read and write so they could protect his interests.
    c. He apprenticed them to tradesmen in the village. He hoped to build a self-sufficient community for himself and his family.
    d. He sent them away to live with a brother in a large city in the north.

49. What change occurred in Wang Lung in the seventh year of his prosperity?
    a. He began to gain weight because he was not working in the fields as much.
    b. He began to get very greedy and mean.
    c. He saw O-lan as ugly and he lost his feelings for her.
    d. He began to get obsessed with the land, and he spent all of his time working in the fields.

50. Cuckoo's comment about Wang Lung only being a farmer angered him. To show his worth, he asked for Lotus.
    a. True
    b. False

51. What happened to Wang Lung?
    a. He contracted a social disease.
    b. He felt guilty and had nightmares.
    c. He became infatuated and forgot his business.
    d. He got scared and went home to O-lan.

Good Earth Multiple Choice Study/Quiz Questions Page 11

Chapters 20-23

52. Who negotiated the bringing of Lotus into Wang Lung's house?
    a. Cuckoo and Wang Lung's uncle's wife did.
    b. The priest from the temple did.
    c. The old woman at the House of Hwang did.
    d. Wang Lung did it himself, to assert his own dominance.

53. How did Wang Lung treat O-lan?
    a. He tried to buy her off with presents.
    b. He told her it was his right as a husband to bring whomever he chose home.
    c. He begged her to understand his needs.
    d. He left her alone because he was ashamed.

54. What was O-lan's reaction to Lotus?
    a. She threatened to leave if Lotus stayed.
    b. She welcomed her, although grudgingly, because she knew she had no other choice.
    c. She avoided her.
    d. She deliberately antagonized her every chance she got.

55. Describe the relationship between O-lan and Cuckoo.
    a. They hated each other and had to be kept apart.
    b. They ignored each other.
    c. They were civil, although not really friendly.
    d. They became friends. O-lan was lonely since Wang Lung was spending all of his time with Lotus, and O-lan wanted some companionship.

56. Wang Lung encouraged Lotus to become friends with his uncle's wife. He knew they were both lonely and thought they would be good company for each other.
    a. True
    b. False

57. What finally made Wang Lung angry with Lotus?
    a. She called his children idiots and filthy.
    b. She ridiculed his love.
    c. She kept comparing his house to another man's where she had lived previously.
    d. She refused to see him when he wanted to see her.

Good Earth Multiple Choice Study/Quiz Questions Page 12

58. What healed Wang Lung's sickness?
    a. He went to the temple and prayed for a week.
    b. O-lan's love and understanding eventually healed him.
    c. Working the land healed him.
    d. He had a long talk with his father, and finally came to understand himself.

59. Why did Wang Lung keep Lotus after he no longer had a sickness for her?
    a. It was socially unacceptable for him to remove her.
    b. His uncle's wife had grown fond of Lotus and treated her as a daughter. She threatened to cause trouble if he removed her.
    c. It was partly to keep her as a toy to be used when he felt like it, and partly to show the villagers he could afford to keep a non-working person in the house.
    d. Lotus begged and pleaded to stay, then demanded a great deal of money if she had to leave. He decided it was cheaper to keep her.

60. What explanation did O-lan give for the eldest son's behavior?
    a. He never had to work the land. He acted like an idle young lord.
    b. His father's lack of attention had affected him emotionally.
    c. The schooling had poisoned his mind and spirit.
    d. He was born under an unfavorable moon.

61. How did Wang Lung propose to control his son?
    a. He sent him to work in the fields.
    b. He wanted to marry him off.
    c. He sent him away to the University.
    d. He gave him a good beating and threatened more if the boy didn't shape up.

62. For what advice did Wang Lung go to Lotus?
    a. He wanted to see if she knew how to make O-lan less angry.
    b. He wanted to see if she knew of anyone who would make a good wife for his son.
    c. He wanted help to invest a large sum of money. He thought he might know of a trustworthy banker.
    d. He wanted to buy new furniture and clothes and wanted her opinion.

63. Who arranged the marriage of the eldest son?
    a. O-lan as mother of the groom made the arrangements.
    b. Wang Lung made the arrangements.
    c. Cuckoo did it because she knew the prospective bride's father.
    d. Lotus made the arrangements.

Good Earth Multiple Choice Study/Quiz Questions Page 13

64. Why did Wang Lung go to see Yang?
    a. He wanted to pay her off to refuse to see his son.
    b. He took her a present from Lotus.
    c. He was tired of Lotus and wanted someone new.
    d. He wanted her to instruct the new bride in the ways of marriage.

65. How did Wang Lung feel about having his uncle's family in his house?
    a. He thought it was good luck to have so many relatives living under one roof.
    b. It was a necessary evil that he had to endure.
    c. He was beginning to like it because having them there distracted O-lan and she didn't bother him.
    d. He wanted them to go because they were a bad influence on his own family.

66. Wang Lung allowed his uncle's family to stay because he discovered that his uncle was an official in a band of robbers. He was afraid that the robbers would destroy his home and harm his family if he didn't let the uncle's family stay.
    a. True
    b. False

Good Earth Multiple Choice Study/Quiz Questions Page 14

Chapters 24-27

67. What did Wang Lung do with his eldest son while waiting for the wedding?
    a. He made him the foreman in the field that was the farthest from the house.
    b. He sent him to a monastery to pray.
    c. He sent him away to school.
    d. He confined him to the house and made him help O-lan with the "women's work."

68. Wang Lung went to see the merchant to ask him to take his second son as an apprentice and to ask if the merchant had a son for his second daughter.
    a. True
    b. False

69. What was his daughter's reply when Wang Lung asked why she wept?
    a. She said she was crying because her brothers were causing so much trouble in the family. Her mother told her not to weep "because you are the lord and master, and can sell me to another house if I cause trouble here when you already have so much sorrow from your sons."
    b. She said she cried because her mother bound her feet, but "my mother said I was not to weep aloud because you are too kind and weak for pain and you might say to leave me as I am, and then my husband would not love me, even as you do not love her."
    c. She said she cried because she was sick. Her mother told her not to weep because "good money is not spent on sickly girls. They are taken to the mountains to die." After that she was afraid to tell anyone how she felt.
    d. She said she wept because she wanted to go away to school and learn, like her brothers. Her mother told her never to mention it "because it is not the place of a woman to learn book things. A woman must cook and clean and bear sons. What man would want a woman who preferred reading and learning over pleasing him?

70. After his children were betrothed, Wang Lung began to fall in love with O-lan again.
    a. True
    b. False

71. What was the doctor's verdict about O-lan's illness?
    a. She would die.
    b. She would get better if she could rest for a few months.
    c. She needed surgery which had to be performed in the city.
    d. There was nothing wrong with her physically. She was emotionally distraught and it was causing physical symptoms.

Good Earth Multiple Choice Study/Quiz Questions Page 15

72. What were O-lan's final words to Cuckoo?
    a. "You, by your evil deeds, have brought shame upon me and caused a sickness to consume my body. The evil spirits will be with you and make you remember your misdeeds."
    b. "Well, and you may have lived in the courts of the Old Lord, and you were accounted beautiful, but I have been a man's wife and I have borne him sons, and you are still a slave."
    c. "You must now make sure that my husband and my sons are attended to. Let them want for nothing."
    d. "I cannot leave this life with hatred on my soul. Although you have wronged me many times, forgiveness is in my heart."

73. What were O-lan's wishes?
    a. She wished that Cuckoo and Lotus would not be allowed in her room or to touch her things when she is gone, and she wished to see her son wed before she died.
    b. She wished that Wang Lung would spend her last days with her, and that he would banish Lotus after she had died.
    c. She wished to have a large funeral procession, fitting of a rich man's wife, and to be buried in the graveyard at the Hwang's house.
    d. She wished that her daughter would be allowed to take her place as mistress of the household, and stay there to take care of Wang Lung instead of being married off. She also wished that all of her things should be buried with her.

74. Were her wishes carried out?
    a. Yes
    b. No

75. By what means did Wang Lung and his son decide to make the uncle's family less of a nuisance?
    a. They bought them their own house in town so they would be far away from Wang Lung's family.
    b. They sent them on a long journey.
    c. They decided to give the family opium.
    d. They started to poison their food in the hopes of slowly killing them.

76. What did Wang Lung do with his daughter to protect her from the nephew?
    a. He kept her at home and hired a bodyguard.
    b. He gave her a knife and told her to use it to protect herself.
    c. He took her to the fields with him every day.
    d. He sent her to live with the family of her future husband.

Good Earth Multiple Choice Study/Quiz Questions Page 16

Chapters 28-30

77. What effect did the great flood have on Wang Lung's fortunes?
   a. He lost everything. The fields were so flooded he couldn't harvest his crops or pay his workers. All of the good topsoil was washed away, and he was left with useless dirt.
   b. He gained in money and social position because he was able to sell his grain at high prices and buy other farmers' land at low prices.
   c. There was no real effect on his future. He was set back for a bit but was able to resume normal operations quickly.
   d. All the money he had hidden in holes on his land was washed away.

78. What did the eldest son suggest doing?
   a. He wanted to sell everything and move to the great city in the north.
   b. He wanted to keep working the fields and get them back in good shape.
   c. He wanted to move into the Hwang home to get away from his cousin.
   d. He wanted to build a mill on some of the land so they could start to grind their own grain, and that of the other farmers. He thought this would make more money for them.

79. The second son wanted a wife who would have a good dowry, be neither too pretty or too plain, be a good cook, and be very thrifty in her use of fabric for clothing.
   a. True
   b. False

80. Where did Wang Lung's nephew go?
   a. He went to school in the south.
   b. He ran off with a band of robbers.
   c. He didn't go anywhere; he stayed around the house and was a nuisance to everyone.
   d. He went off to join the war, to see different parts of the country.

81. Who moved first to the House of Hwang?
   a. Cuckoo and Lotus and the eldest son and his family moved in first.
   b. Wang Lung moved in first with "the poor fool."
   c. The uncle and his wife moved in first.
   d. Lotus and Wang Lung moved in together.

82. When did the rest of the family move in to the Hwang house?
   a. They moved in a year later, as was the custom.
   b. They moved in after Ching died.
   c. They moved in the next day.
   d. They didn't want to move, so they stayed in the old house.

Good Earth Multiple Choice Study/Quiz Questions Page 17

83. Why did the eldest son want to decorate the house so well?
    a. He wanted to give his wife everything she wanted.
    b. He wanted to spend as much of the money as possible so robbers could not steal it.
    c. He wanted to impress the wedding guests.
    d. He thought he was honoring his father by doing so.

84. What was the second son's reaction to the first son's spending?
    a. He didn't like it; he was very thrifty.
    b. He thought it was a great idea.
    c. He didn't care one way or the other. He wasn't interested in the affairs at home.
    d. He returned all the goods he could return.

85. What promise did Wang Lung make to his uncle's wife?
    a. He promised to give her a decent burial.
    b. He promised to take care of his uncle if she should die first.
    c. He promised her an allowance.
    d. He promised to find a wife for her son if he should return.

Good Earth Multiple Choice Study/Quiz Questions Page 18

Chapters 31-34

86. Who came to stay at Wang Lung's Hwang house?
   a. His second daughter and her husband and his younger brother came.
   b. The nephew and some soldiers came.
   c. The uncle's robber friends came.
   d. Some more relatives from the west moved in.

87. What problem occurred at the house?
   a. The visitor was chasing the women.
   b. The visitor was selling Wang Lung's possessions on the black market.
   c. The visitor was terrorizing the children.
   d. The visitor was giving opium to the other members of the household.

88. What did the visitor leave behind?
   a. He left behind a child to the servant girl he used.
   b. He left a bag of gold in payment for his misdeeds.
   c. He left a trail of destruction.
   d. He left nothing but hard feelings.

89. Wang Lung banished the unwed slave woman and her newborn daughter.
   a. True
   b. False

90. Where did Wang Lung's third son want to go?
   a. He wanted to go to the university.
   b. He wanted to go back to the old house.
   c. He wanted to go off to the wars.
   d. He wanted to go to the city in the south to seek his own fortune.

91. The son asked for Pear Blossom. Did Wang Lung grant him his request?
   a. Yes
   b. No

92. How did Wang Lung satisfy Lotus when he took Pear Blossom?
   a. He told her she could entertain other men.
   b. He sent her on a trip to visit her family.
   c. He gave her the material things she wanted.
   d. He bought two more slave girls for her.

Good Earth Multiple Choice Study/Quiz Questions Page 19

93. How did each of Wang Lung's sons react to Wang Lung's having Pear Blossom?
    a. The eldest thought it was disgusting. The second agreed. The third thought he should do as he pleased.
    b. The eldest left the house. The second thought he should do as he pleased. The third said nothing.
    c. The eldest thought he should do as he pleased. The second said nothing. The third left and joined the army.
    d. The first son left and joined the army. The second moved his family to another town. The third said nothing.

94. Why did the third son leave?
    a. He was offered a good job in the city to the south.
    b. He disagreed with his father and felt his father was a hypocrite.
    c. He wanted to go to the university.
    d. He was in love with his brother's wife and knew he had to leave before a scandal occurred.

95. What promise did Pear Blossom make to Wang Lung?
    a. She promised to take care of his eldest girl, "the poor fool," after his death.
    b. She promised to burn incense and put fresh flowers on his grave every month.
    c. She promised to make sure Lotus did not take another husband before one year had ended.
    d. She promised to see that the crops were harvested.

96. Wang Lung went to O-lan's burial site alone when it was time to die.
    a. True
    b. False

97. What would the two remaining sons do after Wang Lung died?
    a. They would sell his land and divide the profits.
    b. They would continue to accumulate his land and begin to build a very wealthy and powerful clan.
    c. They argued over who should control the land, and the younger son killed the older one.
    d. They kicked out Pear Blossom and Lotus.

ANSWER KEY - MULTIPLE CHOICE STUDY/QUIZ QUESTIONS
The Good Earth

Chapters 1-4	Chapters 5-9		Chapters 10-14		Chapters 15-19
1. B	10. A	20. C	28. B	36. A	42. C
2. A	11. A	21. D	29. C	37. B	43. C
3. B	12. B	22. B	30. B	38. C	44. D
4. A	13. B	23. D	31. A	39. C	45. B
5. D	14. A	24. B	32. C	40. B	46. A
6. C	15. B	25. C	33. D	41. A	47. C
7. B	16. B	26. D	34. B		48. B
8. A	17. D	27. A	35. C		49. C
9. A	18. B				50. A
	19. A				51. C

Chapters 20-23	Chapters 24-27	Chapters 28-30	Chapters 31-34
52. A	67. C	77. B	86. B
53. D	68. A	78. C	87. A
54. C	69. B	79. A	88. A
55. A	70. B	80. D	89. B
56. B	71. A	81. A	90. C
57. A	72. B	82. B	91. B
58. C	73. A	83. C	92. C
59. C	74. A	84. A	93. C
60. A	75. C	85. D	94. B
61. B	76. D		95. A
62. B			96. B
63. C			97. A
64. A			
65. D			
66. A			

PREREADING VOCABULARY WORKSHEETS

VOCABULARY - *The Good Earth*

Chapters 1-4
Part I: Using Prior Knowledge and Contextual Clues

    Below are the sentences in which the vocabulary words appear in the text. Read the sentence. Use any clues you can find in the sentence combined with your prior knowledge, and write what you think the underlined words mean on the lines provided.

1. . . . an ox twisted its head from behind the corner next to the door and <u>lowed</u> at him deeply.

___

2. He was <u>supping</u> loudly at his bowl.

___

3. . . . upon a <u>dais</u> in the center of the room he saw a very old lady . . . .

___

4. Wang Lung fell to his knees and knocked his head on the floor. "Raise him," said the old lady gravely to the gatemen, "these <u>obeisances</u> are not necessary."

___

5. She rose and drew about her her loosened garments and fastened them closely about her throat and waist, fitting them to her body with a slow <u>writhe</u> and twist.

___

6. The old man's cough rose <u>querulously</u> out of the dusky dawn . . . .

___

7. . . . for when the sun struck the <u>zenith</u> he could go to his house and food would be there ready for him to eat . . . .

___

8. . . . Wang Lung was <u>frugal</u> and he did not . . . spend his money freely . . . .

___

Good Earth Vocabulary Chapters 1-4 Continued

9. . . . Wang Lung would say, "This is a good dish of noodles," and O-lan would answer in depreciation, "It is good flour we have this year from the fields."

Part II: Match the words to their dictionary definitions.

_____ 1. lowed   A. contortion
_____ 2. supped   B. a raised platform
_____ 3. dais   C. grumblingly; complainingly
_____ 4. obeisances   D. thrifty; tight
_____ 5. writhe   E. mooed
_____ 6. querulously   F. highest point
_____ 7. zenith   G. making less of something
_____ 8. frugal   H. ate
_____ 9. depreciation   I. gestures of homage, deference or reverence

Good Earth Vocabulary Chapters 5-9

Part I: Using Prior Knowledge and Contextual Clues
   Below are the sentences in which the vocabulary words appear in the text. Read the sentence. Use any clues you can find in the sentence combined with your prior knowledge, and write what you think the underlined words mean on the lines provided.

1. As for our son, there was not even a child among the concubines of the Old Master himself to compare to him in beauty and dress.

   _____

2. They said nothing more to each other, but he was pleased, and the incessant bending and stooping seemed less arduous . . . .

   _____

3-4. They united in only one thing and this was to berate the agent for his ill management of the estates, so that he who had once been oily and unctuous, a man of plenty and of ease, was now become anxious and harried . . . .

   _____

   _____

5. From his fields Wang Lung reaped scanty harvest of hardy beans . . . .

   _____

6. His uncle, who was among the first to be hungry, came importuning to his door . . . .

   _____

7. . . . this other one who would, with the cruelty of new and ardent life, steal from the very flesh and blood of its mother.

   _____

8. Once he walked . . . to the temple of the earth and deliberately he spat upon the face of the small imperturbable god who sat there with his goddess.

   _____

Good Earth Vocabulary Chapters 5-9 Continued

II. Determining the Meaning - Match the words to their dictionary definitions.

_____ 1. concubines   A. slick; also characterized by insincere earnestness
_____ 2. arduous   B. persistently pleading
_____ 3. berate   C. women contracted as second wives
_____ 4. unctuous   D. unshakable; calm and steady
_____ 5. reaped   E. passionate; full of strong feeling or enthusiasm
_____ 6. importuning   F. reprimand; scold
_____ 7. ardent   G. harvested; cut and collected
_____ 8. imperturbable H. difficult

Good Earth Vocabulary Chapters 10-14

Part I: Using Prior Knowledge and Contextual Clues
Below are the sentences in which the vocabulary words appear in the text. Read the sentence. Use any clues you can find in the sentence combined with your prior knowledge, and write what you think the underlined words mean on the lines provided.

1. Upon the doorsteps lay <u>cowering</u> a few dingy shapes of men and women who gazed, famished, upon the closed a barred gate . . . .

_____

2. . . . they were pushed somehow in the darkness and in the yelling and crying of many voices into a small open door and into a box-like room, and then with an <u>incessant</u> roaring the thing in which they rode tore forth into the darkness . . . .

_____

3. And men laughed suddenly at the smiling, <u>wizened</u> little old man . . . .

_____

4. . . . first smearing yourself with mud and filth to make yourselves as <u>piteous</u> as you can.

_____

5. . . . and with one mat she had <u>contrived</u> not to use they made a floor and sat down and were sheltered.

_____

6. But another <u>ricksha</u> puller stood near and leaned over as he counted . . . .

_____

7. Clinging thus to the outskirts of the great, sprawling <u>opulent</u> city it seemed that at least there could not be any lack of food.

_____

8. . . . his body <u>clad</u> in what he wore day after day, because there was no quilt to cover him and only a mat upon bricks beneath him.

_____

Good Earth Vocabulary Chapters 10-14 Continued

9. "Well, and but why do they seize my neighbor, who is as innocent as I who have never heard of this new war?" asked Wang Lung in great consternation.

_____

Part II: Determining the Meaning - Match the words to their dictionary definitions.

_____ 1. cowering   A. continuous
_____ 2. incessant   B. deserving pity
_____ 3. wizened   C. having or showing great wealth
_____ 4. piteous   D. a state of paralyzing dismay
_____ 5. contrived   E. withered; wrinkled
_____ 6. ricksha   F. devised; planned; managed
_____ 7. opulent   G. clothed
_____ 8. clad   H. cringing in fear
_____ 9. consternation   I. small two-wheeled carriage pulled by 1 or 2 people

Good Earth Vocabulary Chapters 15-19

Part I: Using Prior Knowledge and Contextual Clues
    Below are the sentences in which the vocabulary words appear in the text. Read the sentence. Use any clues you can find in the sentence combined with your prior knowledge, and write what you think the underlined words mean on the lines provided.

1. And up from the <u>quiescent</u>, waiting land a faint mist rose, . . . and clung about the tree trunks.

_____

2. Then Wang Lung set himself robustly to the soil and he <u>begrudged</u> even the hours he must spend in the house for food and sleep.

_____

3. . . . Wang Lung saw a handsome, <u>shrewish</u>, high-colored face looking out at him.

_____

4. She pursed her narrow red lips <u>virtuously</u> as she spoke these words, and cast down her bold eyes . . . .

_____

5. . . . and when the boy had put it smartly before him and with an <u>impudent</u> gesture had caught and tossed the penny he paid for it, Wang Lung fell to musing.

_____

6. He was <u>compelled</u> to build yet another room to the house to store his harvest in, or they would not have space to walk in the house.

_____

7. He laughed <u>boisterously</u> at what she had done and then he thought of a merry thing to say . . . .

_____

8. . . . it was foolish for him to work when there were those who ate his rice while they were half <u>idle</u> waiting day after day for the waters to recede.

_____

Good Earth Vocabulary Chapters 15-19 Continued

9. Then he heard laughter . . . tinkling as the silver bell upon a <u>pagoda</u> shaking in the wind . . . .

_____

Part II: Determining the Meaning - Match the words to their dictionary definitions.

_____ 1. quiescent   A. ill-humored
_____ 2. begrudged   B. bold and offensive
_____ 3. shrewish   C. inactive; not working; being lazy
_____ 4. virtuously   D. loudly; without restraint
_____ 5. impudent   E. gave reluctantly or resentfully
_____ 6. compelled   F. quiet; still; inactive
_____ 7. boisterously   G. multi-story Buddhist tower
_____ 8. idle   H. showing moral excellence, virtue, or chastity
_____ 9. pagoda   I. forced

Good Earth Vocabulary Chapters 20-23

Part I: Using Prior Knowledge and Contextual Clues
　　Below are the sentences in which the vocabulary words appear in the text. Read the sentence. Use any clues you can find in the sentence combined with your prior knowledge, and write what you think the underlined words mean on the lines provided.

1. . . . Wang Lung sat agape, for he had forgotten that his uncle lived and it was like a dead man returning to see him.

___

2. And it is not for you to repine when he has money and buys himself another to bring her to his house, for all men are so . . . .

___

3. She answered volubly and eagerly.

___

4. So Wang Lung dallied alone in the little new court he had built for Lotus . . . .

___

5. And then she said with a deeper malice, "She is not so young as she looks, my nephew!"

___

6. He would have liked to speak out to say in a surly voice of master, "Well, it is my house and whoever I say may come in, shall come in, and who are you to ask?" But he could not . . . .

___

7. Lotus was fretful and she answered peevishly, pouting her lips and hanging her head away from him.

___

8. Now Lotus, seeing Wang Lung distraught in her presence . . . .

___

Good Earth Vocabulary Chapters 20-23 Continued

9. . . . the sooner the better, and let us marry them as soon as they begin to <u>yearn</u>, for I cannot have this over again three more times!

___

Part II: Determining the Meaning - Match the words to their dictionary definitions.

_____ 1. agape	A. characterized by fluent speech
_____ 2. repine	B. in a state of wonder or amazement
_____ 3. volubly	C. emotionally upset
_____ 4. dallied	D. intent of ill-will
_____ 5. malice	E. in a contrary way; querulously
_____ 6. surly	F. to long for; to have feelings of tenderness for
_____ 7. peevishly	G. be discontented or in low spirits
_____ 8. distraught	H. gruff
_____ 9. yearn	I. tarried; loitered; also means flirted

Good Earth Vocabulary Chapters 24-27

Part I: Using Prior Knowledge and Contextual Clues
  Below are the sentences in which the vocabulary words appear in the text. Read the sentence. Use any clues you can find in the sentence combined with your prior knowledge, and write what you think the underlined words mean on the lines provided.

1. . . . when he turned upon the bed she complained and was petulant and she pushed him away.

___

2. When the eldest son was gone Wang Lung felt the house was purged of some surcharge of unrest and it was a relief to him.

___

3. But he looked at her with some strange remorse, and he saw that she had grown thin and her skin was sere and yellow.

___

4. Now when O-lan heard the words, "five hundred pieces of silver" she came suddenly out of her languor and she said weakly . . . .

___

5. To everything the maid was acquiescent, but reluctant and shy as was proper and correct for her.

___

6. Then Wang Lung was scrupulous to do all that should be done for the one dead . . . .

___

7. And Wang Lung spoke aloud at last, musing . . . .

___

Good Earth Vocabulary Chapters 24-27 Continued

Part II: Determining the Meaning - Match the words to their correct definitions.

_____ 1. petulant   A. passively agreeable
_____ 2. purged   B. bitter regret
_____ 3. remorse   C. conscientious; exact
_____ 4. languor   D. purified; rid of undesirable elements
_____ 5. acquiescent   E. unreasonable ill-tempered
_____ 6. scrupulous   F. considering thoughtfully
_____ 7. musing   G. lack of energy; listlessness

Good Earth Vocabulary Chapters 28-34

Part I: Using Prior Knowledge and Contextual Clues
　　Below are the sentences in which the vocabulary words appear in the text. Read the sentence. Use any clues you can find in the sentence combined with your prior knowledge, and write what you think the underlined words mean on the lines provided.

1. Wang Lung had come in robustly from the fields and in high humor because the water was off the land and the air dry and warm . . . .

_____

2-3. And moved by some strange impulse he went forward and he sat down where she had sat and he put his hand on the table and from the eminence it gave him he looked down on the bleary face of the old hag who blinked at him and waited in silence for what he would do.

_____

_____

4. Then Wang Lung's heart leaped with pleasure but he hid his pleasure artfully and he demurred in pretense . . . .

_____

5. Ever since that day the young maid had been in disfavor with Lotus, and although the girl waited on her silently and slavishly, and stood by her side all day filling her pipe and fetching this and that, ... still Lotus was not satisfied.

_____

6. . . . Lotus was loath to part with her and yet she would part with her, and in this unaccustomed conflict Lotus was the more angry because of her discomfort . . . .

_____

7. Sometimes she looked at Wang Lung, fully and without coquetry as a child does . . . .

_____

Good Earth Vocabulary Chapters 28-34 Continued

Part II: Determining the Meaning - Match the words to their dictionary definitions.

_____ 1. robust   A. blurred and/or reddened
_____ 2. eminence   B. like a slave
_____ 3. bleary   C. position of superiority
_____ 4. demurred   D. flirting
_____ 5. slavishly   E. objected
_____ 6. loath   F. full of strength and energy
_____ 7. coquetry   G. reluctant

ANSWER KEY - VOCABULARY
The Good Earth

Chapters 1-4
1. E
2. H
3. B
4. I
5. A
6. C
7. F
8. D
9. G

Chapters 5-9
1. C
2. H
3. F
4. A
5. G
6. B
7. E
8. D

Chapters 10-14
1. H
2. A
3. E
4. B
5. F
6. I
7. C
8. G
9. D

Chapters 15-19
1. F
2. E
3. A
4. H
5. B
6. I
7. D
8. C
9. G

Chapters 20-23
1. B
2. G
3. A
4. I
5. D
6. H
7. E
8. C
9. F

Chapters 24-27
1. E
2. D
3. B
4. G
5. A
6. C
7. F

Chapters 28-34
1. F
2. C
3. A
4. E
5. B
6. G
7. D

DAILY LESSONS

LESSON ONE

Objectives
1. To introduce *The Good Earth* unit.
2. To distribute books and other related materials
3. To preview the study questions for chapters 1-4
4. To familiarize students with the vocabulary for chapters 1-4

Activity #1

Distribute the materials students will use in this unit. Explain in detail how students are to use these materials.

Study Guides Students should read the study guide questions for each reading assignment prior to beginning the reading assignment to get a feeling for what events and ideas are important in the section they are about to read. After reading the section, students will (as a class or individually) answer the questions to review the important events and ideas from that section of the book. Students should keep the study guides as study materials for the unit test.

Vocabulary Prior to reading a reading assignment, students will do vocabulary work related to the section of the book they are about to read. Following the completion of the reading of the book, there will be a vocabulary review of all the words used in the vocabulary assignments. Students should keep their vocabulary work as study materials for the unit test.

Reading Assignment Sheet You need to fill in the reading assignment sheet to let students know by when their reading has to be completed. You can either write the assignment sheet up on a side blackboard or bulletin board and leave it there for students to see each day, or you can "ditto" copies for each student to have. In either case, you should advise students to become very familiar with the reading assignments so they know what is expected of them.

Extra Activities Center The Extra Activities page of this unit contains suggestions for an extra library of related books and articles in your classroom as well as crossword and word search puzzles. Make an extra activities center in your room where you will keep these materials for students to use. (Bring the books and articles in from the library and keep several copies of the puzzles on hand.) Explain to students that these materials are available for students to use when they finish reading assignments or other class work early.

Nonfiction Assignment Sheet Explain to students that they each are to read at least one non-fiction piece from the in-class library at some time during the unit. Students will fill out a nonfiction assignment sheet after completing the reading to help you evaluate their reading experiences and to help the students think about and evaluate their own reading experiences. Students may use the information they read for the introductory research project to fulfill their nonfiction reading assignment for this unit.

Books Each school has its own rules and regulations regarding student use of school books. Advise students of the procedures that are normal for your school.

Activity #3

Tell students that prior to your next class period they should have previewed the study questions and done the prereading vocabulary worksheet for Chapters 1-4. Students should also have read Chapters 1-4 of *The Good Earth*.

NONFICTION ASSIGNMENT SHEET
(To be completed after reading the required nonfiction article)

Name _____ Date _____

Title of Nonfiction Read _____

Written By _____ Publication Date _____

I. Factual Summary: Write a short summary of the piece you read.

II. Vocabulary
    1. With which vocabulary words in the piece did you encounter some degree of difficulty?

    2. How did you resolve your lack of understanding with these words?

III. Interpretation: What was the main point the author wanted you to get from reading his work?

IV. Criticism
    1. With which points of the piece did you agree or find easy to accept? Why?

    2. With which points of the piece did you disagree or find difficult to believe? Why?

V. Personal Response: What do you think about this piece? <u>OR</u> How does this piece influence your ideas?

LESSON TWO

Objectives
   1. To review the main ideas and events from chapters 1-4
   2. To introduce students to the background research project for this unit
   3. To give students the opportunity to find and read information for the research project

Activity #1
   Give students a few minutes to formulate answers for the study guide questions for chapters 1-4, and then discuss the answers to the questions in detail. Write the answers on the board or overhead transparency so students can have the correct answers for study purposes.
   Note: It is a good practice in public speaking and leadership skills for individual students to take charge of leading the discussions of the study questions. Perhaps a different student could go to the front of the class and lead the discussion each day that the study questions are discussed during this unit. Of course, the teacher should guide the discussion when appropriate and be sure to fill in any gaps the students leave.

Activity #2
   Distribute the Project Assignment Sheet. Discuss the directions in detail. Take your class to your school's library/media center so they may begin working on the project.

LESSON THREE

Objectives
   1. To evaluate students' research
   2. To prepare students for their oral reports
   3. To give students the opportunity to practice writing to inform
   4. To give the teacher the opportunity to evaluate students' writing skills

Activity #1
   Distribute Writing Assignment #1. Discuss the directions in detail. Give students ample time to complete the assignment.

Activity #2
   Tell students that prior to your next class meeting they should have done the prereading and reading work for chapters 5-9.

RESEARCH PROJECT ASSIGNMENT SHEET - *The Good Earth*

PROMPT

You can read *The Good Earth* as a book unto itself without knowing anything else about China. However, the book will be much more meaningful for you if you learn a little bit about China, too.

The purpose of this assignment is to give you the opportunity to learn more about China so you can not only better appreciate the book *The Good Earth*, but also so you can better understand the place of China in our world today and our relationship with that country.

ASSIGNMENT

Each of you will be assigned a topic related to China. Look in books, magazines and/or encyclopedias to find the information you need. Don't forget the possibility that some information may be on video or other media resources.

You will have the remainder of this class time to begin your research. In our next class meeting, you will write a written report about your articles in preparation for an oral report in the following class period(s).

THE PRESENTATION

You will be required to make an oral presentation about the information you find. The presentation does not have to be long, but you do have to let the rest of us know the most important points you found in your reading. Most presentations will probably last 2-5 minutes.

TOPIC

Write down here the topic you have been assigned.

_____

RESEARCH TOPICS ASSIGNMENTS - *The Good Earth*

TOPIC	ASSIGNED TO
PHYSICAL FEATURES/MAP	
NATURAL RESOURCES	
HISTORY TO 1911	
HISTORY 1911-PRESENT	
CULTURE	
GOVERNMENT	
COMMUNISM IN CHINA	
CLIMATE, VEGETATION, ANIMAL LIFE	
PEOPLE	
SOCIETY AND FAMILY	
CITIES	
RELIGION	
LANGUAGE	
ART	
LITERATURE	
SCIENCE/TECHNOLOGY	
EDUCATION	
HEALTH AND WELFARE	
AGRICULTURE	
ECONOMY	
MANUFACTURING	
TRANSPORTATION/ COMMUNICATION	
INTERNATIONAL RELATIONS	
PLACES OF INTEREST	
CURRENT EVENTS (LAST 5 YEARS)	
CURRENT EVENTS (LAST 5 YEARS)	
SPORTS	

WRITING ASSIGNMENT #1 - *The Good Earth*

PROMPT
      You have gathered information about China. Now, write a composition in which you tell about the information you have gathered. Think of this as a script for your oral presentation. By doing this writing assignment, you will gather and organize your facts thus preparing yourself for your oral presentation.

PREWRITING
      You have done most of your prewriting work already by taking notes as you gathered information. Your notes will have a natural flow to them and will probably need little organizing. If you took notes in a haphazard fashion, you will need to organize them so that the ideas flow naturally, one to another.

DRAFTING
      The easiest way to write this composition is to write an introductory paragraph in which you introduce your topic. In the body of your composition, give a summary of the information you gathered, organizing it in a logical fashion so it is easy to understand and follow. Then, write a paragraph in which you give your own response to the information you collected.

PROMPT
      When you finish the rough draft of your paper, ask a student who sits near you to read it. After reading your rough draft, he/she should tell you what he/she liked best about your work, which parts were difficult to understand, and ways in which your work could be improved. Reread your paper considering your critic's comments, and make the corrections you think are necessary.

PROOFREADING
      Do a final proofreading of your paper double-checking your grammar, spelling, organization, and the clarity of your ideas.

LESSON FOUR

Objectives
1. To review the main ideas and events of chapters 5-9
2. To preview and read chapters 10-14
3. To expose all students to a variety of information about China
4. To give students the opportunity to practice public speaking

Activity #1
Give students a few minutes to formulate answers for the study guide questions for chapters 5-9, and then discuss the answers to the questions in detail. Write the answers on the board or overhead transparency so students can have the correct answers for study purposes.

Activity #2
Tell students that prior to Lesson Six (give students a day/date), they should have done the prereading and reading work for chapters 10-14.

Activity #3
Ask each student to give a brief oral report about the nonfiction work he/she read for the research project assignment. Your criteria for evaluating this report will vary depending on the level of your students. You may wish for students to give a complete report without using notes of any kind, or you may want students to read directly from a written report, or you may want to do something in between these two extremes. Just make students aware of your criteria in ample time for them to prepare their reports.

LESSON FIVE

Objectives
1. To expose all students to a wealth of information about China
2. To give students the opportunity to practice their public speaking skills

Activity
Continue the oral presentations begun in Lesson Four as described there.

LESSON SIX

Objectives
1. To review the main ideas and events of chapters 10-14
2. To conclude the oral reports
3. To preview and read chapters 15-19

Activity #1

Give students a few minutes to formulate answers for the study guide questions for chapters 10-14, and then discuss the answers to the questions in detail. Write the answers on the board or overhead transparency so students can have the correct answers for study purposes.

Activity #2

Tell students that prior to your next class meeting they should have done the prereading and reading work for chapters 15-19. If time remains in this class period after the oral presentations have concluded, students may work on this assignment.

Activity #3

Continue and conclude the oral reports about China.

LESSON SEVEN

Objectives
1. To review the main ideas and events from chapters 15-19
2. To preview and read chapters 20-23
3. To evaluate students' oral reading skills

Activity # 1

Give students a few minutes to formulate answers for the study guide questions for chapters 15-19, and then discuss the answers to the questions in detail. Write the answers on the board or overhead transparency so students can have the correct answers for study purposes.

Activity #2

Give students about ten to fifteen minutes to preview the study questions and do the prereading vocabulary work for chapters 20-23.

Activity #3

Have students read chapters 20-23 of *The Good Earth* out loud in class. You probably know the best way to get readers with your class; pick students at random, ask for volunteers, or use whatever method works best for your group. If you have not yet completed an oral reading evaluation for your students this marking period, this would be a good opportunity to do so. A form is included with this unit for your convenience.

If students do not complete reading chapters 20-23 in class, they should do so prior to your next class meeting.

ORAL READING EVALUATION - *The Good Earth*

ame _____ Class_____ Date _____

SKILL	EXCELLENT	GOOD	AVERAGE	FAIR	POOR
Fluency	5	4	3	2	1
Clarity	5	4	3	2	1
Audibility	5	4	3	2	1
Pronunciation	5	4	3	2	1
_____	5	4	3	2	1
_____	5	4	3	2	1

Total ____   Grade ____

Comments:

LESSON EIGHT

Objectives
1. To review the main ideas and events for chapters 20-23
2. To preview and read chapters 24-27
3. To get students to think about the extra material that was presented
4. To give students the opportunity to express their personal opinions
5. To give the teacher the opportunity to evaluate students' writing skills
6. To help prepare students for the second project that goes along with this unit

Activity #1

Give students a few minutes to formulate answers for the study guide questions for chapters 20-23, and then discuss the answers to the questions in detail. Write the answers on the board or overhead transparency so students can have the correct answers for study purposes.

Activity #2

Tell students that prior to your next class meeting they should have completed the prereading and reading work for chapters 24-27. If they finish the writing assignment early, they may begin this reading assignment.

Activity #3

Distribute Writing Assignment #2. Discuss the directions in detail and give students ample time to complete the assignment.

LESSON NINE

Objectives
1. To review the main ideas and events of chapters 24-27
2. To preview and read chapters 28-30
3. To evaluate students' oral reading skills

Activity #1

Give students a few minutes to formulate answers for the study guide questions for chapters 24-27, and then discuss the answers to the questions in detail. Write the answers on the board or overhead transparency so students can have the correct answers for study purposes.

Activity #2

Give students about fifteen minutes to preview the study questions and do the vocabulary work for chapters 28-30.

Activity #3

Have students read chapters 28-30 orally in class. Continue the oral reading evaluations. Tell students that this assignment must be completed prior to your next class meeting.

WRITING ASSIGNMENT #2 - *The Good Earth*

PROMPT

You have heard and read a great many facts relating to China, and you have had some time to think about those facts. Now you are to turn into a roving reporter, getting opinions from others about the information you have all heard.

Your assignment is to write down five questions. The questions must prompt the person you are asking to give a personal opinion about the information reported in class about China. Each question should focus on a different aspect of the information presented.

After you write down your questions, go interview three of your classmates (separately), ask each of the three classmates all five questions, and write down their responses.

PREWRITING

Most of your prewriting has been done through your reading and the oral reports; you have information about which to ask questions. Review your notes from the oral reports. Make a list of topics that were covered in the reports. Think about each topic. Brainstorm a list of questions related to those topics.

Look through your list of topics and decide which ones will provoke an opinion as an answer. Put a star next to those questions. Which of the starred questions will prompt the most interesting responses from the people you interview? Circle those questions. Choose five of the circled questions to use for your interviews. Your questions must require more than "Yes" or "No" answers.

Find a classmate who is available to be interviewed. Ask him/her your five questions and write down his/her answers. When you finish with one interview, go to another student and do another interview. Interview a total of three classmates, and then review your notes prior to drafting.

DRAFTING

Put your usual heading at the top of your paper. Write down the first question you asked. Under that, write the responses from each of the three people you interviewed. Write one good paragraph for each response. Label each response: "Response 1," "Response 2," and "Response 3." Repeat this pattern for each of the questions you asked and responses you received.

PROOFREADING

When you finish the rough draft of your composition, ask a student who sits near you to read it. After reading your rough draft, he/she should tell you what he/she liked best about your work, which parts were difficult to understand, and ways in which your work could be improved. Reread your paper considering your critic's comments, and make the corrections you think are necessary. Do a final proofreading of your paper double-checking your grammar, spelling, organization, and the clarity of your ideas.

LESSON TEN

Objectives
1. To review the main ideas and events from chapters 28-30
2. To preview and read chapters 31-34

Activity #1
Give students a few minutes to formulate answers for the study guide questions for chapters 28-30, and then discuss the answers to the questions in detail. Write the answers on the board or overhead transparency so students can have the correct answers for study purposes.

Activity #2
Give students about fifteen minutes to preview the study questions and do the vocabulary work for chapters 31-34.

Activity #3
Have students read chapters 31-34 orally in class. Complete the oral reading evaluations if you have not yet done so. If your oral reading evaluations are complete, students may read this assignment silently or in groups. Tell students that this assignment must be completed prior to your next class meeting.

LESSON ELEVEN

Objectives
1. To review the main ideas and events from chapters 31-34
2. To discuss *The Good Earth* on interpretive and critical levels

Activity #1
Take a few minutes at the beginning of the period to review the study questions for chapters 31-34.

Activity #2
Choose the questions from the Extra Discussion Questions/Writing Assignments which seem most appropriate for your students. A class discussion of these questions is most effective if students have been given the opportunity to formulate answers to the questions prior to the discussion. To this end, you may either have all the students formulate answers to all the questions, divide your class into groups and assign one or more questions to each group, or you could assign one question to each student in your class. The option you choose will make a difference in the amount of class time needed for this activity.

Activity #3
After students have had ample time to formulate answers to the questions, begin your class discussion of the questions and the ideas presented by the questions. Be sure students take notes during the discussion so they have information to study for the unit test.

EXTRA WRITING ASSIGNMENTS/DISCUSSION QUESTIONS - *The Good Earth*

Interpretation
1. From what point of view is *The Good Earth* written? What advantages did using that point of view give the author?

2. If you were to rewrite *The Good Earth* as a play, where would you start and end each act? Explain why.

3. Where is the climax of the story? Explain your choice.

4. What are the main conflicts in the novel? Are they all resolved? If so, how? If not, why not?

Critical
6. Who were the six women in the story who affected (and were affected by) Wang Lung? For what purpose(s) did he need each?

7. Are Wang Lung's actions believably motivated? Explain why or why not.

8. Explain the importance of the setting in *The Good Earth*. Could this story have been set in a different time and place and still have the same effect?

9. Characterize Pearl Buck's style of writing. How does it contribute to the value of the novel?

10. Discuss the validity of using the city as a "bad" place and the country as a "good" place.

11. Explain how the title relates to the events of the novel and the themes of *The Good Earth*.

12. Explain the relationship between the House of Hwang and the House of Wang.

16. Are the characters in *The Good Earth* stereotypes? If so, explain why Pearl Buck used stereotypes. If not, explain how the characters merit individuality.

17. Compare and contrast the House of Wang and the House of Hwang.

18. Compare and contrast the birth of Wang Lung's first son with the birth of his second son and his grandson.

19. What is the symbolic importance of each of the following: Wang Lung's braid, the land, feet, the colors red and black, and water?

The Good Earth Extra Discussion Questions page 2

20. After the seven years of prosperity, Wang Lung suffers a series of family troubles. What is each problem he faced, and what was the solution to each?

21. Compare Wang Lung's wedding to his first son's wedding.

22. Compare and contrast Wang Lung's sons.

23. Contrast Wang Lung's sons' reactions to his relationship with Pear Blossom and explain how each son's reaction is consistent with his character.

24. Compare city life today with city life in *The Good Earth*.

25. Compare and contrast Wang Lung with his sons.

26. What was the role of religion in Wang Lung's life?

27. Several times in the novel Wang Lung appears to be a hypocrite. Explain when, how and why.

28. Explain the role of education in the novel. Is it good or bad?

29. What were the outward signs of a wealthy family?

30. In the end, was Wang Lung's family different from Hwang's? How so, or why not?

31. There were certain things Wang Lung would not do or felt guilty doing even though they were customary. What were those things, and why did he feel guilty or not do them?

32. What purpose did O-lan's death serve in the whole context of the novel?

33. Why will the sons sell the land and divide the profits?

Personal Response

34. Suppose Pearl Buck had left out the part about the sons' selling the land and dividing the profits. How would that have changed the theme(s) of the book?

35. Did you enjoy reading *The Good Earth*? Why or why not?

36. Was Wang Lung a good husband and father?

37. Would you like to visit China? Why or why not?

LESSON TWELVE

Objective
    To review all of the vocabulary work done in this unit

Activity
    Choose one (or more) of the vocabulary review activities listed below and spend your class period as directed in the activity. Some of the materials for these review activities are located in the Extra Activities in this unit.

VOCABULARY REVIEW ACTIVITIES

1. Divide your class into two teams and have an old-fashioned spelling or definition bee.

2. Give each of your students (or students in groups of two, three or four) a *Good Earth* Vocabulary Word Search Puzzle. The person (group) to find all of the vocabulary words in the puzzle first wins.

3. Give students a *Good Earth* Vocabulary Word Search Puzzle without the word list. The person or group to find the most vocabulary words in the puzzle wins.

4. Use a *Good Earth* Vocabulary Crossword Puzzle. Put the puzzle onto a transparency on the overhead projector (so everyone can see it), and do the puzzle together as a class.

5. Give students a *Good Earth* Vocabulary Matching Worksheet to do.

6. Divide your class into two teams. Use the *Good Earth* vocabulary words with their letters jumbled as a word list. Student 1 from Team A faces off against Student 1 from Team B. You write the first jumbled word on the board. The first student (1A or 1B) to unscramble the word wins the chance for his/her team to score points. If 1A wins the jumble, go to student 2A and give him/her a definition. He/she must give you the correct spelling of the vocabulary word which fits that definition. If he/she does, Team A scores a point, and you give student 3A a definition for which you expect a correctly spelled matching vocabulary word. Continue giving Team A definitions until some team member makes an incorrect response. An incorrect response sends the game back to the jumbled-word face off, this time with students 2A and 2B. Instead of repeating giving definitions to the first few students of each team, continue with the student after the one who gave the last incorrect response on the team. For example, if Team B wins the jumbled-word face-off, and student 5B gave the last incorrect answer for Team B, you would start this round of definition questions with student 6B, and so on. The team with the most points wins!

7. Have students write a story in which they correctly use as many vocabulary words as possible. Have students read their compositions orally! Post the most original compositions on your bulletin board!

LESSON THIRTEEN

Objectives
1. To give students the opportunity to practice writing to persuade
2. To give the teacher the opportunity to evaluate students' writing skills
3. To have students prepare materials that will be used in the unit project

Activity

Distribute Writing Assignment #3. Discuss the directions in detail and give students ample time to complete the assignment.

While students are working on this assignment, call individual students to your desk or some other private area for a writing conference based on the first two writing assignments in this unit. An evaluation form is provided to help structure your conferences.

LESSONS FOURTEEN - SEVENTEEN

Objectives
1. To bring together all the elements students have been studying in this unit
2. To review the ideas in the unit
3. To give students practical experience in organizing and presenting information
4. To give students practice comparing, contrasting and evaluating information

Activity #1

Distribute the Unit Project Assignment and discuss the directions in detail.

TEACHER NOTES:

The length of time this project takes will depend on the level of your students and how involved you decide you want to get.

This unit plan is based on using Lesson Fourteen as a planning session in which students decide what types of things and what format they wish to use in their video. Lesson Fifteen would be used for students to write scripts and compile the appropriate materials. Lesson Sixteen would be a working session to finalize the scripts, rehearse and/or begin filming. Lesson Seventeen would be for filming, and Lesson Eighteen would be for viewing the film.

You might want to decide what students will put in the film (or what structure they will use) if you have a lower level class. Middle and upper level classes should be able to devise their own format. This unit assumes you have a middle or upper level class.

The earlier part of this unit was designed to create ample materials for students to use and edit for this video. Students have piles of factual information from research and Writing Assignment #1. They have opinions about all of those topics from Writing Assignment #2, with which they might have a "man on the street" interview section on the video. Finally, Writing Assignment #3 provides students with the material for short, educational "commercials" between their stories, interviews, etc. Encourage the use of visual aids, graphics, pictures, costumes, props, etc.

WRITING ASSIGNMENT #3 - *The Good Earth*

PROMPT

Every day you are bombarded with a sea of persuasive arguments ranging from parents trying to get you out of bed and off to school ("I've told you three times to get up and get ready for school; now get up or else . . . ."), to teachers trying to get you to pay attention and do your work ("Pay attention! There will be a quiz next week, and you had better know this information!"), to coaches persuading you to give your best efforts at practice ("You guys had better shape up and put forth some effort if you hope to beat _____ on Friday night!), to businesses trying to get you and your parents to buy their products (Commercials on television and radio are great examples of persuasive arguments.)

There are other more subtle forms of persuasion -- a look from a friend that says, "If you don't do this, you're definitely not cool," a slanted news story that gives only one side of the story making that side appear to be right, a little comment here or there that helps to form your opinions about an issue, a person, or an idea, and so on. Many times we don't even recognize the fact that we are being manipulated (That's what persuasion is--manipulation!).

You can never practice the art of persuasion too much. It's like practicing magic or a card trick. You can learn to do it so well that the person or people you are persuading will never know they are being persuaded, just like the audience never knows how the magician did the trick. Why? Why would you want to have this skill? Think about it. Imagine always getting your own way, having people do what you want them to do without much of an argument. You've heard of "the art of persuasion"; there is another saying: "the power of persuasion." If you are good at the art of persuasion, you have power.

Your assignment is to write a script for a television commercial (30 seconds long) relating to China. For example, you could do a commercial enticing tourists to come to China. Other topics could be to protect the endangered species found in China or to purchase some item that is made in China. Think of a topic that interests you; you don't have to use one of these ideas.

PREWRITING

Choose a topic about which you want to do your commercial. Answer these questions: What is the purpose of the commercial? Who is the audience? Of what am I going to persuade the audience? What is most likely to persuade them? Make a list of the things that would be likely to persuade your audience. Circle your best ideas. Jot down notes about how each could be incorporated into your commercial. If something won't fit in, decide whether or not it is important enough to devise a way to keep it in, or if it would be just as well left out. Make a little outline description of your commercial.

DRAFTING

Under the heading PURPOSE, state the purpose of your commercial. Under the heading MATERIALS, make a list of props/materials needed to create the commercial. Under the heading ACTION, describe your commercial as you see the finished product. Under the heading MISCELLANEOUS, put in any notes, comments, or directions -- or anything that you feel is important to mention but won't fit in the other headings.

PROOFREADING

When you finish the rough draft of your commercial, ask a student who sits near you to read it. After reading your rough draft, he/she should tell you what he/she liked best about your work, which parts were difficult to understand, and ways in which your work could be improved. Reread your paper considering your critic's comments, and make the corrections you think are necessary.

Do a final proofreading of your paper double-checking your grammar, spelling, organization, and the clarity of your ideas.

WRITING EVALUATION FORM - *The Good Earth*

Name _____ Date _____

Grammar: excellent   good   fair   poor

Spelling: excellent   good   fair   poor

Punctuation: excellent   good   fair   poor

Legibility: excellent   good   fair   poor

Strengths:

Weaknesses:

Comments/Suggestions:

UNIT PROJECT ASSIGNMENT - *The Good Earth*

PROMPT

You have done a great deal of work in this unit finding out about China, and you have accumulated considerable knowledge on the topic. It's time to share the wealth. Other classes of students in history or social studies, for example, often study China. (Who knows? Perhaps such a study in another class is in *your* future!) Given a choice between going to the library and digging out the information as you have done, or watching a great video that tells you everything you would need to know, which would you choose? . . . . Thought so! So you are going to create a video that includes everything a person needs to know about China.

REQUIREMENTS

The video must last between 40 and 50 minutes.
It must include basic facts about China (location, topography, climate, population, culture, natural resources, etc.)
It must include some history of China.
It must include current issues in China.
Everyone in the class must contribute to the video, and everyone must participate in the creation of the video.

GETTING STARTED

1. Decide on a basic format.

What kind of a video would you like to watch? A video with someone like Dan Rather sitting at a desk reading off facts or a teacher standing in the front of the room lecturing? Or would you prefer to watch a video that has humor, action, music, and presents the material in an interesting way? Detail what kinds of ideas pop into your head, and make a list.

2. Decide on what categories of information must be covered in the video.

Make a list of the categories of information that need to be included. Next to each category, make a little list of ideas about how that information could be presented.

3. Consider the information you already have created and gathered through the three writing assignments in this unit.

Make notes about ways you could use the materials and facts you have already created. You have basic facts, opinions, and persuasive commercials already composed on a variety of topics.

4. Combine and summarize your thoughts from 1-3 above. Come to definite decisions about what should be in the video and how it should be presented. Make a list of things that will be included and next to the items, make notes about how they will be presented. Assign each item an amount of time in which it must be presented in the video. The most important items should have the most time, and the least important items should have the least time.

5. Make a list of things that need to be done.

Start with the first item on your list from 4. above. Make a list of specific tasks that must be done to get ready for filming this segment. Make a list of props needed, if any. Do this for each item on the list, and then assign one person to do each task. (A task may be writing a script, making a map, creating a costume, or anything that needs to be done.) Read the list of props needed, and see who can bring items to class. Decide where and how to make or get the items no one in class has readily available.

6. Do the tasks. Make sure everyone knows what needs to be done, what he/she is expected to do, and by when each task must be completed. Then rehearse and film.

LESSON NINETEEN

Objective
>To review the main ideas presented in *The Good Earth*

Activity #1
>Choose one of the review games/activities included in this guide and spend your class period as outlined there. Some materials for these activities are located in the Extra Activities section of this unit.

Activity #2
>Remind students that the Unit Test will be in the next class meeting. Stress the review of the Study Guides and their class notes as a last minute, brush-up review for homework.

REVIEW GAMES/ACTIVITIES - *The Good Earth*

1. Ask the class to make up a unit test for *The Good Earth*. The test should have 4 sections: matching, true/false, short answer, and essay. Students may use 1/2 period to make the test and then swap papers and use the other 1/2 class period to take a test a classmate has devised. (open book) You may want to use the unit test included in this guide or take questions from the students' unit tests to formulate your own test.

2. Take 1/2 period for students to make up true and false questions (including the answers). Collect the papers and divide the class into two teams. Draw a big tic-tac-toe board on the chalk board. Make one team X and one team O. Ask questions to each side, giving each student one turn. If the question is answered correctly, that students' team's letter (X or O) is placed in the box. If the answer is incorrect, no mark is placed in the box. The object is to get three marks in a row like tic-tac-toe. You may want to keep track of the number of games won for each team.

3. Take 1/2 period for students to make up questions (true/false and short answer). Collect the questions. Divide the class into two teams. You'll alternate asking questions to individual members of teams A & B (like in a spelling bee). The question keeps going from A to B until it is correctly answered, then a new question is asked. A correct answer does not allow the team to get another question. Correct answers are +2 points; incorrect answers are -1 point.

4. Have students pair up and quiz each other from their study guides and class notes.

5. Give students a *Good Earth* crossword puzzle to complete.

6. Divide your class into two teams. Use the *Good Earth* crossword words with their letters jumbled as a word list. Student 1 from Team A faces off against Student 1 from Team B. You write the first jumbled word on the board. The first student (1A or 1B) to unscramble the word wins the chance for his/her team to score points. If 1A wins the jumble, go to student 2A and give him/her a clue. He/she must give you the correct word which matches that clue. If he/she does, Team A scores a point, and you give student 3A a clue for which you expect another correct response. Continue giving Team A clues until some team member makes an incorrect response. An incorrect response sends the game back to the jumbled-word face off, this time with students 2A and 2B. Instead of repeating giving clues to the first few students of each team, continue with the student after the one who gave the last incorrect response on the team. For example, if Team B wins the jumbled-word face-off, and student 5B gave the last incorrect answer for Team B, you would start this round of clue questions with student 6B, and so on. The team with the most points wins!

UNIT TESTS

SHORT ANSWER UNIT TEST 1 - *The Good Earth*

I. Matching/Identify

_____ 1. Wang Lung   A. Author

_____ 2. Blossom   B. Wang Lung bought land from the House of ____

_____ 3. Buck   C. Belonged to a band of robbers

_____ 4. Cuckoo   D. Materialistic; eggs were dyed red for this person

_____ 5. Hwang   E. Had a strong attachment to the land

_____ 6. Lotus   F. Servant with whom Wang Lung bargained for land

_____ 7. Olan   G. Wang Lung's first mistress

_____ 8. Uncle   H. Went to join the war and see the country

_____ 9. Nephew   I. Promised to take care of Wang Lung's daughter

_____ 10. First Son   J. Wang Lung's wife

II. Short Answer

1. What do we learn about Wang Lung as we see him making preparations for his wedding day?

2. Why did Wang Lung say that O-lan was "a woman such as is not commonly found"?

3. Why did Wang Lung's uncle and uncle's wife have an "evil destiny"?

4. How was Wang Lung different from the other poor men around him in the city?

Good Earth Short Answer Unit Test 1 Page 2

5. Why did Wang Lung send his sons to school?

6. What sickness did Wang Lung get?

7. Why did Wang Lung allow his uncle's family to stay?

8. What effect did the great flood have on Wang Lung's fortunes?

9. Why did Wang Lung take his family South?

10. What did the two remaining sons do after Wang Lung died?

Good Earth Short Answer Unit Test 1 Page 3

III. Essay

Wang Lung said, "If you sell the land, it is the end." What did he mean? Explain using examples from the book and relating your answer to the themes in the book.

The Good Earth Short Answer Unit Test 1 Page 4

IV. Vocabulary

    Listen to the vocabulary words and spell them. After you have spelled all the words, go back and write down the definitions.

1.

2.

3.

4.

5.

6.

7.

8.

9.

10.

SHORT ANSWER UNIT TEST 2 - *The Good Earth*

I. Matching/Identify

_____ 1. Wang Lung   A. Went to join the war and see the country

_____ 2. Blossom   B. Promised to take care of Wang Lung's daughter

_____ 3. Buck   C. Wang Lung's wife

_____ 4. Cuckoo   D. Had a strong attachment to the land

_____ 5. Hwang   E. Materialistic; eggs were dyed red for this person

_____ 6. Lotus   F. Wang Lung's first mistress

_____ 7. O-lan   G. Servant with whom Wang Lung bargained for land

_____ 8. Uncle   H. Author

_____ 9. Nephew   I. Wang Lung bought land from the House of ____

_____ 10. First Son   J. Belonged to a band of robbers

II. Short Answer

1. Describe Wang Lung's social position on his wedding day and contrast that with his social position at the time of his death.

2. Of what had Wang Lung's Hwang parcel of land become a symbol?

3. How was the delivery and acceptance of the second boy different from the first?

Good Earth Short Answer Unit Test 2 Page 2

4. "He lived in the rich city as alien as a rat in a rich man's house that is fed on scraps thrown away, and hides here and there and is never a part of the real life of the house." Who was Pearl Buck describing?

5. Selling a female child into slavery was a commonly accepted means of survival for the poor. Why didn't Wang Lung sell his baby girl?

6. What difference between Wang Lung and the crowd does Wang Lung's innocent question, "Sir, is there any way whereby the rich who oppress us can make it rain so that I can work on the land" show us?

7. What change occurred in Wang Lung in the seventh year of his prosperity?

8. Why did Wang Lung keep Lotus after he no longer had a sickness for her?

9. After his children were betrothed, how did Wang Lung's opinion (view) of O-lan change?

10. By what means did Wang Lung and his son decide to make the uncle's family less of a nuisance?

11. What effect did the great flood have on Wang Lung's fortunes?

12. How did each of Wang Lung's sons react to Wang Lung's having Pear Blossom?

Good Earth Short Answer Unit Test 2 Page 3

III. Composition

1. What purpose does O-lan's death serve in the context of the whole novel and its themes?

2. How is Wang Lung different from his sons?

3. Describe Wang Lung's relationship(s) with each of the six females in the book.

The Good Earth Short Answer Unit Test 2 page 4

IV. Vocabulary

    Listen to the vocabulary word and spell it. After you have spelled all the words, go back and write down the definition.

1.

2.

3.

4.

5.

6.

7.

8.

9.

10.

KEY: SHORT ANSWER UNIT TESTS - *The Good Earth*

The short answer questions are taken directly from the study guides.
If you need to look up the answers, you will find them in the study guide section.

Answers to the composition questions will vary depending on your
class discussions and the level of your students.

For the vocabulary section of the test, choose ten of the
words from the vocabulary lists to read orally for your students.

The answers to the matching section of the test are below.

Answers to the matching section of the Advanced Short Answer Unit Test
are the same as for Short Answer Unit Test #2.

Test #1	Test #2
1. E	1. D
2. I	2. B
3. A	3. H
4. F	4. G
5. B	5. I
6. G	6. F
7. J	7. C
8. C	8. J
9. H	9. A
10. D	10. E

ADVANCED SHORT ANSWER UNIT TEST - *The Good Earth*

I. Matching/Identify

_____ 1. Wang Lung   A. Went to join the war and see the country

_____ 2. Blossom   B. Promised to take care of Wang Lung's daughter

_____ 3. Buck   C. Wang Lung's wife

_____ 4. Cuckoo   D. Had a strong attachment to the land

_____ 5. Hwang   E. Materialistic; eggs were dyed red for this person

_____ 6. Lotus   F. Wang Lung's first mistress

_____ 7. O-lan   G. Servant with whom Wang Lung bargained for land

_____ 8. Uncle   H. Author

_____ 9. Nephew   I. Wang Lung bought land from the House of ____

_____ 10. First Son   J. Belonged to a band of robbers

II. Short Answer

1. Describe Wang Lung's relationship(s) with each of the six females in the story.

   a.

   b.

   c.

   d.

   e.

   f.

Good Earth Advanced Short Answer Unit Test Page 2

2. Discuss how Pearl Buck uses the city/wealth versus land/poverty as a theme in *The Good Earth*.

3. Explain how the title relates to the events of the novel and the themes of *The Good Earth*.

4. Explain the relationship between the House of Hwang and the House of Wang.

5. What is the symbolic importance of each of the following: Wang Lung's braid, the land, feet, the colors red and black, and water?

6. Compare and contrast Wang Lung's sons.

Good Earth Advanced Short Answer Unit Test Page 3

7. How is Wang Lung different from his sons?

8. Explain the role of education in the novel. Is it good or bad?

9. What purpose did O-lan's death serve in the whole context of the novel?

10. Why will the sons sell the land and divide the profits?

The Good Earth Advanced Short Answer Unit Test page 4

III. Composition
The New York Times said of *The Good Earth*, "A comment upon the meaning and tragedy of life as it is lived in any age in any quarter of the globe." Defend that statement using specific examples from the book *The Good Earth*.

The Good Earth Advanced Short Answer Unit Test page 5

IV. Vocabulary

Listen to the vocabulary words and write them down. After you have written down all the words, write a paragraph using all of the vocabulary words. The paragraph must in some way relate to *The Good Earth*.

MULTIPLE CHOICE UNIT TEST 1 - *The Good Earth*

I. Matching/Identify

_____ 1. Wang Lung   A. Author

_____ 2. Blossom   B. Wang Lung bought land from the House of ____

_____ 3. Buck   C. Belonged to a band of robbers

_____ 4. Cuckoo   D. Materialistic; eggs were dyed red for this person

_____ 5. Hwang   E. Had a strong attachment to the land

_____ 6. Lotus   F. Servant with whom Wang Lung bargained for land

_____ 7. Olan   G. Wang Lung's first mistress

_____ 8. Uncle   H. Went to join the war and see the country

_____ 9. Nephew   I. Promised to take care of Wang Lung's daughter

_____ 10. First Son   J. Wang Lung's wife

II. Multiple Choice

1. Describe Wang Lung's entrance into the House of Hwang on his wedding day.
    a. He is calm and confident, and is treated with respect by the gateman.
    b. He approaches with fear and apprehension, and the gateman treats him roughly.
    c. He enters acting as if he is already the master of the house, which was the custom.
    d. He attempts to enter, but he is turned away at the gate.

2. Which of the following does not describe O-Lan?
    a. She is very pretty.
    b. She is tall.
    c. She is calm and quiet.
    d. She possesses a great deal of inner strength.

3. Why did Wang-Lung say that O-lan was "a woman such as is not commonly found"?
    a. She could read and write, although she rarely told people that she could.
    b. She did all of her usual jobs until it was time to deliver the baby. After the birth, she cleaned everything up herself.
    c. He was amazed that she got pregnant as quickly as she did, and made sure she had a son for her first born.
    d. She could do as much work as a man and still be a pretty and loving wife.

Good Earth Multiple Choice Unit Test 1 Page 2

4. Why were the cakes and the visit to the house of Hwang important?
    a. The cakes and the son's attire were an outward sign to the Hwang family of Wang Lung's prosperity. He could return to the house of Hwang as a little more than a very poor farmer, and in this he took pride.
    b. In the superstitious religion of the simple farmers, they insured the newborn's place in the hereafter.
    c. Since they were the richest family in the area, they could demand that any child they wanted be brought to them. This was Wang Lung's way of showing that he could give them money in return for the privilege of keeping his child.
    d. He was very superstitious. He thought that showing respect to the rich family would bring good fortune on his son.

5. Wang Lung's purchase of the Hwang parcel of land became symbolic of his growing greed and materialism.
    a. True
    b. False

6. Why did Wang Lung's uncle and uncle's wife have an "evil destiny"?
    a. His uncle was the third child born in the third month of the third day. This was considered to be very unlucky.
    b. They were lazy and shiftless, and brought most of their misfortunes on themselves.
    c. His uncle's wife had been injured as a young woman, and was not well. She was considered a jinx on the rest of the family.
    d. His uncle did not believe in the power of the gods. The religious people of the village thought this was the cause of his problems.

7. What did Wang Lung do to try and find food and work?
    a. He asked for work at the temple but was turned away.
    b. He went south.
    c. He went out at night, looking for scraps in people's trash.
    d. He offered a sacrifice to the gods and begged for help.

8. How did Pearl Buck aptly describe Wang Lung's life in the city?
    a. ". . . as a rat in a rich man's house"
    b. ". . . as a fish out of water"
    c. ". . . as a fly in honey"
    d. ". . . as a maggot on the good earth"

9. Selling a female child into slavery was a commonly accepted means of survival for the poor. Did Wang Lung sell his baby girl?
    a. Yes, he did so gladly to get rid of the bad luck.
    b. No, he could not part with her.
    c. Yes, he did so, but with great hesitation.
    d. No, he couldn't get enough money for her to make it worthwhile.

Good Earth Multiple Choice Unit Test 1 Page 3

10. How was Wang Lung different from the other poor men around him in the city?
    a. He had land and knew the value of it.
    b. He had brought his family with him.
    c. He was the only man from the north, and still had his braid of hair.
    d. He was the only one who spoke his dialect.

11. What change occurred in Wang Lung in the seventh year of his prosperity?
    a. He began to gain weight because he was not working in the fields as much.
    b. He began to get very greedy and mean.
    c. He saw O-lan as ugly and he lost his feelings for her.
    d. He began to get obsessed with the land, spending all of his time working in the fields.

12. What was O-lan's reaction to Lotus?
    a. She threatened to leave if Lotus stayed.
    b. She welcomed her, although grudgingly, because she knew she had no other choice.
    c. She avoided her.
    d. She deliberately antagonized her every chance she got.

13. What finally made Wang Lung angry with Lotus?
    a. She called his children idiots and filthy.
    b. She ridiculed his love.
    c. She kept comparing his house to another man's where she had lived previously.
    d. She refused to see him when he wanted to see her.

14. What healed Wang Lung's sickness?
    a. He went to the temple and prayed for a week.
    b. O-lan's love and understanding eventually healed him.
    c. Working the land healed him.
    d. He had a long talk with his father, and finally came to understand himself.

15. Why did Wang Lung keep Lotus after he no longer had a sickness for her?
    a. It was socially unacceptable for him to remove her.
    b. His uncle's wife had grown fond of Lotus and treated her as a daughter. She threatened to cause trouble if he removed her.
    c. It was partly to keep her as a toy to be used when he felt like it, and partly to show the villagers he could afford to keep a non-working person in the house.
    d. Lotus begged and pleaded to stay, then demanded a great deal of money if she had to leave. He decided it was cheaper to keep her.

Good Earth Multiple Choice Unit Test 1 Page 4

16. What was his daughter's reply when Wang Lung asked why she wept?
    a. She said she was crying because her brothers were causing so much trouble in the family.
    b. She said she cried because her mother bound her feet, but "my mother said I was not to weep aloud because you are too kind and weak for pain and you might say to leave me as I am, and then my husband would not love me, even as you do not love her."
    c. She said she cried because she was sick. Her mother told her not to weep because "good money is not spent on sickly girls. They are taken to the mountains to die."
    d. She said she wept because she wanted to go away to school and learn, like her brothers. Her mother told her never to mention it "because it is not the place of a woman to learn book things. A woman must cook and clean and bear sons."

17. What were O-lan's final words to Cuckoo?
    a. "You, by your evil deeds, have brought shame upon me and caused a sickness to my body. The evil spirits will be with you and make you remember your misdeeds."
    b. "... you may have lived in the courts of the Old Lord, and you were accounted beautiful, but I have been a man's wife and I have borne him sons, and you are still a slave."
    c. "You must now make sure that my husband and my sons are attended to. Let them want for nothing."
    d. "I cannot leave this life with hatred on my soul. Although you have wronged me many times, forgiveness is in my heart."

18. What effect did the great flood have on Wang Lung's fortunes?
    a. He lost everything. The fields were so flooded he couldn't harvest his crops or pay his workers. All of the good topsoil was washed away, and he was left with useless dirt.
    b. He gained in money and social position because he was able to sell his grain at high prices and buy other farmers' land at low prices.
    c. There was no real effect on his future. He was set back for a bit but was able to resume normal operations quickly.
    d. All the money he had hidden in holes on his land was washed away.

19. How did each of Wang Lung's sons react to Wang Lung's having Pear Blossom?
    a. The eldest thought it was disgusting. The second agreed. The third thought he should do as he pleased.
    b. The eldest left the house. The second thought he should do as he pleased. The third said nothing.
    c. The eldest thought he should do as he pleased. The second said nothing. The third left and joined the army.
    d. The first son left and joined the army. The second moved his family to another town. The third said nothing.

Good Earth Multiple Choice Unit Test 1 Page 5

20. What would the two remaining sons do after Wang Lung died?
    a. They would sell his land and divide the profits.
    b. They would continue to accumulate his land and begin to build a very wealthy and powerful clan.
    c. They argued over who should control the land, and the younger son killed the older one.
    d. They kicked out Pear Blossom and Lotus.

The Good Earth Multiple Choice Unit Test 1 Page 6

III. Composition
    Explain why the title *The Good Earth* is so appropriate for this book. Use specific examples from the book to support your ideas.

The Good Earth Multiple Choice Unit Test 1 Page 7

IV. Vocabulary - Match the correct definitions to the words.

____ 1. VOLUBLY   A. Loudly; without restraint

____ 2. CLAD   B. Devised; planned; managed

____ 3. IMPUDENT   C. Clothed

____ 4. BERATE   D. Gave reluctantly or resentfully

____ 5. CONTRIVED   E. Cringing in fear

____ 6. MALICE   F. Reluctant

____ 7. SUPPED   G. Showing moral excellence, virtue or chastity

____ 8. MUSING   H. Considering thoughtfully

____ 9. BOISTEROUSLY   I. Intent of ill-will

____ 10. DEPRECIATION   J. Bold and offensive

____ 11. AGAPE   K. Making less of something

____ 12. LOWED   L. Difficult

____ 13. VIRTUOUSLY   M. In a state of wonder or amazement

____ 14. CONSTERNATION N. Reprimand; scold

____ 15. BEGRUDGED   O. Mooed

____ 16. LOATH   P. Grumblingly; complainingly

____ 17. ARDUOUS   Q. A state of paralyzing dismay

____ 18. COWERING   R. Characterized by fluent speech

____ 19. QUERULOUSLY   S. Ate

____ 20. EMINENCE   T. Position of superiority

MULTIPLE CHOICE UNIT TEST 2 - *The Good Earth*

I. Matching/Identify

_____ 1. Wang Lung   A. Went to join the war and see the country

_____ 2. Blossom   B. Promised to take care of Wang Lung's daughter

_____ 3. Buck   C. Wang Lung's wife

_____ 4. Cuckoo   D. Had a strong attachment to the land

_____ 5. Hwang   E. Materialistic; eggs were dyed red for this person

_____ 6. Lotus   F. Wang Lung's first mistress

_____ 7. O-lan   G. Servant with whom Wang Lung bargained for land

_____ 8. Uncle   H. Author

_____ 9. Nephew   I. Wang Lung bought land from the House of ____

_____ 10. First Son   J. Belonged to a band of robbers

II. Multiple Choice

1. Describe Wang Lung's entrance into the House of Hwang on his wedding day.
   a. He approaches with fear and apprehension, and the gateman treats him roughly.
   b. He is calm and confident, and is treated with respect by the gateman.
   c. He attempts to enter, but he is turned away at the gate.
   d. He enters acting as if he is already the master of the house, which was the custom.

2. Which of the following does not describe O-Lan?
   a. She is calm and quiet.
   b. She is tall.
   c. She is very pretty.
   d. She possesses a great deal of inner strength.

3. Why did Wang-Lung say that O-lan was "a woman such as is not commonly found"?
   a. He was amazed that she got pregnant as quickly as she did, and made sure she had a son for her first born.
   b. She could do as much work as a man and still be a pretty and loving wife.
   c. She could read and write, although she rarely told people that she could.
   d. She did all of her usual jobs until it was time to deliver the baby. After the birth, she cleaned everything up herself.

Good Earth Multiple Choice Unit Test 2 Page 2

4. Why were the cakes and the visit to the house of Hwang important?
    a. In the superstitious religion of the simple farmers, they insured the newborn's place in the hereafter.
    b. The cakes and the son's attire were an outward sign to the Hwang family of Wang Lung's prosperity. He could return to the house of Hwang as a little more than a very poor farmer, and in this he took pride.
    c. He was very superstitious. He thought that showing respect to the rich family would bring good fortune on his son.
    d. Since they were the richest family in the area, they could demand that any child they wanted be brought to them. This was Wang Lung's way of showing that he could give them money in return for the privilege of keeping his child.

5. Wang Lung's purchase of the Hwang parcel of land became symbolic of his growing greed and materialism.
    a. True
    b. False

6. Why did Wang Lung's uncle and uncle's wife have an "evil destiny"?
    a. They were lazy and shiftless, and brought most of their misfortunes on themselves.
    b. His uncle was the third child born in the third month of the third day. This was considered to be very unlucky.
    c. His uncle did not believe in the power of the gods. The religious people of the village thought this was the cause of his problems.
    d. His uncle's wife had been injured as a young woman, and was not well. She was considered a jinx on the rest of the family.

7. What did Wang Lung do to try and find food and work?
    a. He offered a sacrifice to the gods and begged for help.
    b. He asked for work at the temple but was turned away.
    c. He went out at night, looking for scraps in people's trash.
    d. He went south.

8. How did Pearl Buck aptly describe Wang Lung's life in the city?
    a. ". . . as a fly in honey"
    b. ". . . as a fish out of water"
    c. ". . . as a rat in a rich man's house"
    d. ". . . as a maggot on the good earth"

9. Selling a female child into slavery was a commonly accepted means of survival for the poor. Did Wang Lung sell his baby girl?
    a. No, he could not part with her.
    b. No, he couldn't get enough money for her to make it worthwhile.
    c. Yes, he did so, but with great hesitation.
    d. Yes, he did so gladly to get rid of the bad luck.

Good Earth Multiple Choice Unit Test 2 Page 3

10. How was Wang Lung different from the other poor men around him in the city?
    a. He had brought his family with him.
    b. He had land and knew the value of it.
    c. He was the only man from the north, and still had his braid of hair.
    d. He was the only one who spoke his dialect.

11. What change occurred in Wang Lung in the seventh year of his prosperity?
    a. He saw O-lan as ugly and he lost his feelings for her.
    b. He began to get very greedy and mean.
    c. He began to gain weight because he was not working in the fields as much.
    d. He began to get obsessed with the land, spending all of his time working in the fields.

12. What was O-lan's reaction to Lotus?
    a. She avoided her.
    b. She threatened to leave if Lotus stayed.
    c. She welcomed her, although grudgingly, because she knew she had no other choice.
    d. She deliberately antagonized her every chance she got.

13. What finally made Wang Lung angry with Lotus?
    a. She ridiculed his love.
    b. She refused to see him when he wanted to see her.
    c. She kept comparing his house to another man's where she had lived previously.
    d. She called his children idiots and filthy.

14. What healed Wang Lung's sickness?
    a. He went to the temple and prayed for a week.
    b. Working the land healed him.
    c. O-lan's love and understanding eventually healed him.
    d. He had a long talk with his father, and finally came to understand himself.

15. Why did Wang Lung keep Lotus after he no longer had a sickness for her?
    a. Lotus begged and pleaded to stay, then demanded a great deal of money if she had to leave. He decided it was cheaper to keep her.
    b. His uncle's wife had grown fond of Lotus and treated her as a daughter. She threatened to cause trouble if he removed her.
    c. It was socially unacceptable for him to remove her.
    d. It was partly to keep her as a toy to be used when he felt like it, and partly to show the villagers he could afford to keep a non-working person in the house.

Good Earth Multiple Choice Unit Test 2 Page 4

16. What was his daughter's reply when Wang Lung asked why she wept?
    a. She said she was crying because her brothers were causing so much trouble in the family.
    b. She said she cried because she was sick. Her mother told her not to weep because "good money is not spent on sickly girls. They are taken to the mountains to die."
    c. She said she cried because her mother bound her feet, but "my mother said I was not to weep aloud because you are too kind and weak for pain and you might say to leave me as I am, and then my husband would not love me, even as you do not love her."
    d. She said she wept because she wanted to go away to school and learn, like her brothers. Her mother told her never to mention it "because it is not the place of a woman to learn book things. A woman must cook and clean and bear sons."

17. What were O-lan's final words to Cuckoo?
    a. "... you may have lived in the courts of the Old Lord, and you were accounted beautiful, but I have been a man's wife and I have borne him sons, and you are still a slave."
    b. "I cannot leave this life with hatred on my soul. Although you have wronged me many times, forgiveness is in my heart."
    c. "You, by your evil deeds, have brought shame upon me and caused a sickness to my body. The evil spirits will be with you and make you remember your misdeeds."
    d. "You must now make sure that my husband and my sons are attended to. Let them want for nothing."

18. What effect did the great flood have on Wang Lung's fortunes?
    a. He lost everything. The fields were so flooded he couldn't harvest his crops or pay his workers. All of the good topsoil was washed away, and he was left with useless dirt.
    b. There was no real effect on his future. He was set back for a bit but was able to resume normal operations quickly.
    c. He gained in money and social position because he was able to sell his grain at high prices and buy other farmers' land at low prices.
    d. All the money he had hidden in holes on his land was washed away.

19. How did each of Wang Lung's sons react to Wang Lung's having Pear Blossom?
    a. The eldest thought it was disgusting. The second agreed. The third thought he should do as he pleased.
    b. The eldest left the house. The second thought he should do as he pleased. The third said nothing.
    c. The first son left and joined the army. The second moved his family to another town. The third said nothing.
    d. The eldest thought he should do as he pleased. The second said nothing. The third left and joined the army.

Good Earth Multiple Choice Unit Test 2 Page 5

20. What would the two remaining sons do after Wang Lung died?
    a. They kicked out Pear Blossom and Lotus.
    b. They would sell his land and divide the profits.
    c. They argued over who should control the land, and the younger son killed the older one.
    d. They would continue to accumulate his land and begin to build a very wealthy and powerful clan.

The Good Earth Multiple Choice Unit Test 2 Page 6

III. Composition

1. Compare and contrast Wang Lung and his sons.

2. Wang Lung said, "If you sell the land, it is the end." What did he mean?

3. Explain why the title of the book *The Good Earth* is appropriate.

The Good Earth Multiple Choice Unit Test 2 Page 7

IV. Vocabulary - Match the correct definitions to the words.

    ____ 1. EMINENCE   A. A raised platform

    ____ 2. OBEISANCE   B. In a state of wonder or amazement

    ____ 3. PEEVISHLY   C. In a contrary way; querulously

    ____ 4. VIRTUOUSLY   D. Intent of ill-will

    ____ 5. DEPRECIATION   E. Lack of energy; listlessness

    ____ 6. CONSTERNATION   F. Tarried; loitered; also means flirted

    ____ 7. DISTRAUGHT   G. Making less of something

    ____ 8. AGAPE   H. Showing moral excellence, virtue or chastity

    ____ 9. FRUGAL   I. Considering thoughtfully

    ____ 10. ACQUIESCENT   J. Ate

    ____ 11. DAIS   K. Contortion

    ____ 12. LANGUOR   L. Gestures of homage, deference or reverence

    ____ 13. MALICE   M. Reluctant

    ____ 14. DALLIED   N. A state of paralyzing dismay

    ____ 15. LOATH   O. Position of superiority

    ____ 16. SUPPED   P. Women contracted as second wives

    ____ 17. WRITHE   Q. Emotionally upset

    ____ 18. YEARN   R. Thrifty; tight with money

    ____ 19. MUSING   S. To long for; to have feelings of tenderness for

    ____ 20. CONCUBINES   T. Passively agreeable

ANSWER SHEET - *The Good Earth*
Multiple Choice Unit Tests

I. Matching	II. Multiple Choice	IV. Vocabulary
1. ___	1. ___	1. ___
2. ___	2. ___	2. ___
3. ___	3. ___	3. ___
4. ___	4. ___	4. ___
5. ___	5. ___	5. ___
6. ___	6. ___	6. ___
7. ___	7. ___	7. ___
8. ___	8. ___	8. ___
9. ___	9. ___	9. ___
10. ___	10. ___	10. ___
	11. ___	11. ___
	12. ___	12. ___
	13. ___	13. ___
	14. ___	14. ___
	15. ___	15. ___
	16. ___	16. ___
	17. ___	17. ___
	18. ___	18. ___
	19. ___	19. ___
	20. ___	20. ___

ANSWER KEY - *The Good Earth*
Multiple Choice Unit Tests

Answers to Unit Test 1 are in the left column. Answers to Unit Test 2 are in the right column.

I. Matching	II. Multiple Choice	IV. Vocabulary
1. E D	1. B A	1. R O
2. I B	2. A C	2. C L
3. A H	3. B D	3. J C
4. F G	4. A B	4. N H
5. B I	5. B B	5. B G
6. G F	6. B A	6. I N
7. J C	7. B D	7. S Q
8. C J	8. A C	8. H B
9. H A	9. B A	9. A R
10. D E	10. A B	10. K T
	11. C A	11. M A
	12. C A	12. O E
	13. A D	13. G D
	14. C B	14. Q F
	15. C D	15. D M
	16. B C	16. F J
	17. B A	17. L K
	18. B C	18. E S
	19. C D	19. P I
	20. A B	20. T P

UNIT RESOURCE MATERIALS

BULLETIN BOARD IDEAS - *The Good Earth*

1. Save one corner of the board for the best of students' *The Good Earth* writing assignments.

2. Take one of the word search puzzles from the extra activities and with a marker copy it over in a large size on the bulletin board. Write the clue words to find to one side. Invite students prior to and after class to find the words and circle them on the bulletin board.

3. Write several of the most significant quotations from the book onto the board on brightly colored paper.

4. Make a bulletin board listing the vocabulary words for this unit. As you complete sections of the novel and discuss the vocabulary for each section, write the definitions on the bulletin board. (If your board is one students face frequently, it will help them learn the words.)

5. Place a map of China on the board for use as reference during the oral reports related to China.

6. Make a time line history of China and post that on the bulletin board.

7. Title the board LIVING WITH THE LAND. Post pictures and articles about farming techniques and pictures showing good lands and barren lands.

8. Tell each person that he/she must contribute something to the bulletin board relevant to his/her topic. Have each person post his/her item(s) on the board and explain the significance of each.

9. Post pictures of China from magazines like *National Geographic* or others.

10. Make a travel bulletin board about China. See your local travel agent for pictures, brochures, etc.

11. Title the board THE GOOD EARTH: FEEDING THE HUNGRY. Post information about agencies and ways people are trying to help those who need food.

EXTRA ACTIVITIES

One of the difficulties in teaching a novel is that all students don't read at the same speed. One student who likes to read may take the book home and finish it in a day or two. Sometimes a few students finish the in-class assignments early. The problem, then, is finding suitable extra activities for students.

The best thing I've found is to keep a little library in the classroom. For this unit on *The Good Earth*, you might check out from the school library other related books and articles about farming, buying land, feeding the hungry in the world, history of China, current events in China, careers in agriculture, the jewel and gem industry, Pearl Buck, or articles of criticism about *The Good Earth*.

Other things you may keep on hand are puzzles. We have made some relating directly to *The Good Earth* for you. Feel free to duplicate them.

Some students may like to draw. You might devise a contest or allow some extra-credit grade for students who draw characters or scenes from *The Good Earth*. Note, too, that if the students do not want to keep their drawings you may pick up some extra bulletin board materials this way. If you have a contest and you supply the prize (a CD or something like that perhaps), you could, possibly, make the drawing itself a non-returnable entry fee.

The pages which follow contain games, puzzles and worksheets. The keys, when appropriate, immediately follow the puzzle or worksheet. There are two main groups of activities: one group for the unit; that is, generally relating to *The Good Earth* text, and another group of activities related strictly to *The Good Earth* vocabulary.

Directions for these games, puzzles and worksheets are self-explanatory. The object here is to provide you with extra materials you may use in any way you choose.

MORE ACTIVITIES - *The Good Earth*

1. Pick a chapter or scene with a great deal of dialogue and have the students act it out on a stage. (Perhaps you could assign various scenes to different groups of students so more than one scene could be acted and more students could participate.)

2. Have students design a book cover (front and back and inside flaps) for *The Good Earth.*

3. Have students design a bulletin board (ready to be put up; not just sketched) for *The Good Earth.*

4. Use some of the related topics mentioned earlier for an in-class library as topics for guest speakers.

5. Have students make a diary for Wang Lung. They should make fifteen entries as Wang Lung would have made them. They should choose ten days (or events) which most affected his life and make an entry for each one.

6. Have your students discuss ways (and implement them when possible) that people can help feed the hungry in their own communities and in the world.

7. Use the passage on the following page as a review for grammar or a review for sentence structure. Have students circle the conjunctions and identify the parts they are connecting, have students diagram the sentences, have students identify all the parts of speech in one paragraph, have students rewrite the passage without conjunctions (or with a limited number of conjunctions) to see the difference in how the passage reads, or have students explain the use of writing this passage in this style.

8. Have a "China Day" in which you have students dress in the native costumes, play oriental music, eat native foods, and learn about the different customs related to the different people in China.

GRAMMAR WORKSHEET
The Good Earth

    A great shout went up from those who listened, but Wang Lung turned away unsatisfied. Yes, but there was the land. Money and food are eaten and gone, and if there is not sun and rain in proportion, there is again hunger. Nevertheless, he took willingly the papers the young man gave him, because he remembered that O-lan had never enough paper for the shoe soles, and so he gave them to her when he went home, saying,

    "Now there is some stuff for the shoe soles," and he worked as before.

    But of the men in the huts with whom he talked at evening there were many who heard eagerly what the young man said, the more eagerly because they knew that over the wall there dwelt a rich man and it seemed a small thing that between them and his riches there was only this layer of bricks, which might be torn down with a few knocks of a stout pole, such as they had, to carry their heavy burdens every day upon their shoulders.

    And to the discontent of the spring there was now added the new discontent which the young man and others like him spread abroad in the spirits of the dwellers in the huts, the sense of unjust possession by others of those things which they had not. And as they thought day after day on all these matters and talked of them in the twilight, and above all as day after day their labor brought no added wage, there arose in the hearts of the young and the strong a tide as irresistible as the tide of the river, swollen with winter snows--the tide of the fullness of savage desire.

    But Wang Lung, although he saw this and he heard the talk and felt their anger with a strange unease, desired nothing but his land under his feet again.

    Then in this city out of which something new was always springing at him, Wang Lung saw another new thing he did not understand. He saw one day, when he pulled his ricksha empty down a street looking for a customer, a man ,seized as he stood by a small band of armed soldiers, and when the man protested, the soldiers brandished knives in his face, and while Wang Lung watched in amazement, another was seized and another, and it came to Wang Lung that those who were seized were all common fellows who worked with their hands, and while he stared, yet another man was seized, and this one a man who lived in the hut nearest his own against the wall.

    Then Wang Lung perceived suddenly out of his astonishment that all these men seized were as ignorant as he as to why they were thus being taken, willy nilly, whether they would or not. And Wang Lung thrust his ricksha into a side alley and he dropped it and darted into the door of a hot water shop lest he be next and there he hid, crouched low behind the great cauldrons, until the soldiers passed. And then he asked the keeper of the hot water shop the meaning of this thing he had seen, and the man, who was old and shriveled with the steam rising continually about him out of the copper cauldrons of his trade, answered with indifference.

WORD SEARCH - *The Good Earth*

All words in this list are associated with *The Good Earth*. The words are placed backwards, forward, diagonally, up and down. The included words are listed below the word search.

```
Z R S B M Q F B L S S L C R Q X J B T H Y W R R
T Q K S V J D Q T A T W N C G M R U F E T P H K
X V P K R I B S Z S N F Y T N L R Y G Z E A V W
S O U T H M U N C L E D K F J S U T O L I F E Y
K O T G Q K P H C H U Y Y D G M L H Q T Y H M M
F W L F S C I D R O O M C G H N W E H Z P O J C
L U P D Z N L W R O T O E F X W L T W E N F B L
L Y R L A T I P G E B J L S O L A N N E B U C K
C R Y N N P B D L S S B E Z O E Y N Y C J B B Y
L B X I I J V R I K S L E V D L L S G H B Z V Q
S Z A C M T K B A O L O O R L R D W Y L M K N J
W R H U K D U O X I T Z N V S Z A I C U C K O O
T G I Q E F M R N V D S T F E N C T E H R J F M
F P Y K S Y Q G E C S G K K G P L D N R J N Q C
O V O S L A V E L D T S Y L W B B L O S S O M X
H H G V V T Z L O S H W U T Q C Y Z M R X D B P
C Q T N X H X O V C B N G X Q X V L C V D N D W
F P P H R Q L V E Z G D B C Z J W V R Q F M P W
P V W F N F T E Q H G X R J F R G M Y X W J C Z
X D S B W Y L V R P V P V H T V L B D P N X J G
```

BEG	FLOOD	MEAT	SELLING
BLOSSOM	FURNITURE	MONEY	SLAVE
BRAID	HID	NEPHEW	SOLD
BUCK	HWANG	OLAN	SOLDIERS
CHINA	IDIOTS	OPIUM	SON
CHOKED	JEWELS	OX	SOUTH
CUCKOO	LAND	PROUD	TRAIN
DEATH	LIFE	RAT	UGLY
EGGS	LOTUS	ROBBERS	UNCLE
FEET	LOVE	SCHOOL	WANGLUNG

CROSSWORD - *The Good Earth*

CROSSWORD CLUES - *The Good Earth*

ACROSS

1. A great ___ came; water disaster
4. Direction WL wanted to go to find food and work
7. Author
8. Every one; every bit
9. O-lan bound her daughter's ___
11. Working on it made WL well again
12. Pretend; WL and O-lan --- as if their child is a female with smallpox
15. She married Wang Lung
16. WL sent his sons there to learn to read and write
19. O-lan had ___ hidden in the cloth
22. Transportation south
23. Lotus called WL's children this
25. WL wants to --- all the Hwang land to his own.
26. 'He lived in the rich city as alien as a _ in a rich man's house.'
27. 'When I return to that house it will be with my --- in my arms.'
29. WL's father would not do this
32. In the 7th year of prosperity, WL saw O-lan as ___
34. Characteristic of Wang Lung; he was ___
36. The uncle belonged to a band of ___
38. Place WL & family go in the south; opposite of country
39. Myself
40. ___ a female child was an accepted means of survival for the poor
41. WL & family ---- to the south; go
42. To be allowed or permitted to
43. They arrested poor men

DOWN

2. When WL cut off his braid, O-lan said 'You have cut off your ___!'
3. O-lan killed it for food
4. The two sons ___ WL's land and divided the profits
5. Wang Lung bought land from the House of ___
6. Servant woman with whom WL bargained for land
9. WL sold his ___ to get money to go south
10. Wang Lung dyed these red and gave them to friends to celebrate the birth of his son
11. WL was ___-sick for Lotus
13. O-lan ___ the newborn child; it would have died of starvation
14. WL claimed their child was a female with smallpox & prayed for its ___.
17. Setting for the story
18. WL gave his uncle's family this to make them less of a nuisance
20. Wand Lung's first mistress
21. To escape the soldiers, WL --- during the day
24. WL gave his uncle ___ to protect his own reputation
28. He went to join the war & see the country
29. She promised to take care of Wang Lung's daughter
30. WL cut off his
31. WL would not eat the ___ his 2nd son stole
32. Wang Lung's ___'s family stayed at his house
33. Allow
35. Put off until later
37. O-lan's final words to Cuckoo: '.. you are still a ___'

CROSSWORD ANSWER KEY - *The Good Earth*

MATCHING QUIZ/WORKSHEET 1 - *The Good Earth*

____ 1. SON   A. WL cut off his

____ 2. OPIUM   B. Wang Lung bought land from the House of ___

____ 3. FEET   C. Author

____ 4. PROUD   D. WL would not eat the ___ his 2nd son stole

____ 5. SELLING   E. The two sons ___ WL's land and divided the profits

____ 6. SOLD   F. He had a strong attachment to land

____ 7. FLOOD   G. 'When I return to that house it will be with my --- in my arms.'

____ 8. CHINA   H. She married Wang Lung

____ 9. BUCK   I. Wang Lung's ___'s family stayed at his house

____ 10. BRAID   J. WL's father would not do this

____ 11. WANG LUNG   K. O-lan bound her daughter's ___

____ 12. OLAN   L. O-lan killed it for food

____ 13. TRAIN   M. A great ___ came; water disaster

____ 14. UNCLE   N. Setting for the story

____ 15. HWANG   O. 'He lived in the rich city as alien as a ___ in a rich man's house.'

____ 16. OX   P. Transportation south

____ 17. RAT   Q. ___ a female child was an accepted means of survival for the poor

____ 18. BEG   R. Characteristic of Wang Lung; he was ___

____ 19. MEAT   S. WL gave his uncle's family this to make them less of a nuisance

____ 20. FURNITURE   T. WL sold his ___ to get money to go south

MATCHING QUIZ/WORKSHEET 2 - *The Good Earth*

____ 1. BRAID   A. O-lan killed it for food

____ 2. FEET   B. Author

____ 3. BEG   C. WL gave his uncle's family this to make them less of a nuisance

____ 4. FURNITURE   D. She married Wang Lung

____ 5. IDIOTS   E. ___ a female child was an accepted means of survival for the poor

____ 6. LAND   F. Working on it made WL well again

____ 7. OX   G. O-lan had ___ hidden in the cloth

____ 8. CUCKOO   H. WL sold his ___ to get money to go south

____ 9. OLAN   I. WL's father would not do this

____ 10. CHOKED   J. Setting for the story

____ 11. SLAVE   K. O-lan's final words to Cuckoo: '.. you are still a ___'

____ 12. SOLDIERS   L. O-lan bound her daughter's ___

____ 13. SELLING   M. They arrested poor men

____ 14. CHINA   N. WL cut off his

____ 15. LOTUS   O. To escape the soldiers, WL --- during the day

____ 16. BUCK   P. Wand Lung's first mistress

____ 17. JEWELS   Q. Lotus called WL's children this

____ 18. OPIUM   R. WL was ___-sick for Lotus

____ 19. HID   S. O-lan ___ the newborn child; it would have died of starvation

____ 20. LOVE   T. Servant woman with whom WL bargained for land

KEY: MATCHING QUIZ/WORKSHEETS - *The Good Earth*

Worksheet 1	Worksheet 2
1. G	1. N
2. S	2. L
3. K	3. I
4. R	4. H
5. Q	5. Q
6. E	6. F
7. M	7. A
8. N	8. T
9. C	9. D
10. A	10. S
11. F	11. K
12. H	12. M
13. P	13. E
14. I	14. J
15. B	15. P
16. L	16. B
17. O	17. G
18. J	18. C
19. D	19. O
20. T	20. R

JUGGLE LETTER REVIEW GAME CLUE SHEET - *The Good Earth*

SCRAMBLED	WORD	CLUE
GEB	BEG	WL's father would not do this
SLOBMOS	BLOSSOM	She promised to take care of Wang Lung's daughter
RIDAB	BRAID	WL cut off his ___
KUBC	BUCK	Author
INCHA	CHINA	Setting for the story
KOHDEC	CHOKED	O-lan ___ the newborn child; it would have died of starvation
COOUKC	CUCKOO	Servant woman with whom WL bargained for land
HEADT	DEATH	WL claimed their child was a female with smallpox & prayed for its ___.
GSEG	EGGS	Wang Lung dyed these red and gave them to friends to celebrate the birth of his son.
EFTE	FEET	O-lan bound her daughter's ___
OLDOF	FLOOD	A great ___ came; water disaster
TRUERIFNU	FURNITURE	WL sold his ___ to get money to go south
DIH	HID	To escape the soldiers, WL --- during the day
GAWNH	HWANG	Wang Lung bought land from the House of ___
SOIDIT	IDIOTS	Lotus called WL's children this
LESWEJ	JEWELS	O-lan had ___ hidden in the cloth
DLAN	LAND	Working on it made WL well again
FILE	LIFE	When WL cut off his braid, O-lan said, 'You have cut off your ___!'
OLSUT	LOTUS	Wang Lung's first mistress
VOLE	LOVE	WL was ___-sick for Lotus
TAME	MEAT	WL would not eat the ___ his 2nd son stole
YEONM	MONEY	WL gave his uncle ___ to protect his own reputation
HNPWEE	NEPHEW	He went to join the war & see the country
NOLA	OLAN	She married Wang Lung
IMPUO	OPIUM	WL gave his uncle's family this to make them less of a nuisance
XO	OX	O-lan killed it for food
DROPU	PROUD	Characteristic of Wang Lung; he was ___
TAR	RAT	'He lived in the rich city as alien as a ___ in a rich man's house.'
SEBORBR	ROBBERS	The uncle belonged to a band of ___
COLSOH	SCHOOL	WL sent his sons there to learn to read and write
GELINLS	SELLING	___ a female child was an accepted means of survival for the poor
VALES	SLAVE	O-lan's final words to Cuckoo: '.. you are still a ___'
LODS	SOLD	The two sons ___ WL's land and divided the profits
ROLEDISS	SOLDIERS	They arrested poor men
OSN	SON	'When I return to that house it will be with my --- in my arms.'
HOSUT	SOUTH	Direction WL wanted to go to find food and work
INRAT	TRAIN	Transportation south
GULY	UGLY	In the 7th year of prosperity, WL saw O-lan as ___
CULEN	UNCLE	Wang Lung's ___'s family stayed at his house
UAGGNNLW	WANG LUNG	He had a strong attachment to land

VOCABULARY RESOURCE MATERIALS

VOCABULARY WORD SEARCH - *The Good Earth*

All words in this list are associated with *The Good Earth* with an emphasis on the vocabulary words chosen for study in the text. The words are placed backwards, forward, diagonally, up and down. The included words are listed below.

```
A R D U O U S Z L F J D K Y H D A D B Y L J Z L
R E A P E D E G D U R G E B E R A T E L D I S K
X B H P E N E A B E N O P G D A E L N W E U D Y
Z T A T I C I P M I N T B E R E R P C E O A E M
F G J T I S N O R R H E N U E U V N I U L L R H
A C H P L R R E O E C T Z E S V P I T N B U D Y
O D O W P S W U N I C S A I D T I C R A E T P V
D B O N E O G F L I T I V O W U N S B T P F R O
Z A E G C N Z A R H M M A G L U P R H Y N Y K P
K Y L I A U M N Q U D E N T V F U M L L L O T D
P W Y L S P B U S Y G I S J I T G S I S Y R C B
C E D F I A I N U N A H H R O U Z U V D Y U I
C G T F B E N R N U P A L E R O N O T E L Y N S
Z O W U S G D C T E H P P R R E L Y L H L C L R
R Q Q C L L R R E S S M E E Y U W L S B E N S F
J C E U V A O Q K S I X T D R W E I U S Q M T B
P N X C E P N C D M Y S D E W P V L S B C R C Y
T M K V M T I T F B I Z U K M A O A K H N K K X
K Q G I Z R R Q W O Q Q V O L V N B L L F D L Q
P I T E O U S Y B V V D C S V T D E M U R R E D
```

AGAPE	DALLIED	MUSING	ROBUST
ARDENT	DEMURRED	OBEISANCE	SHREWISH
ARDUOUS	DEPRECIATION	OPULENT	SLAVISHLY
BEGRUDGED	EMINENCE	PAGODA	SUPPED
BERATE	FRUGAL	PEEVISHLY	SURLY
BLEARY	IDLE	PETULANT	UNCTUOUS
BOISTEROUSLY	IMPERTURBABLE	PITEOUS	VOLUBLY
CLAD	IMPORTUNING	PURGED	WIZENED
COMPELLED	IMPUDENT	QUERULOUSLY	WRITHE
CONCUBINES	INCESSANT	QUIESCENT	YEARN
CONTRIVED	LANGUOR	REAPED	ZENITH
COQUETRY	LOATH	REMORSE	
COWERING	LOWED	REPINE	
DAIS	MALICE	RICKSHA	

VOCABULARY CROSSWORD - *The Good Earth*

VOCABULARY CROSSWORD CLUES - *The Good Earth*

ACROSS

2. Gave reluctantly or resentfully
6. Tarried; loitered; also means flirted
10. Inactive; not working; being lazy
12. Prefix meaning 'three'
13. Bold and offensive
14. Clothed
15. 'When I return to that house it will be with my --- in my arms.'
17. O-lan killed it for food
18. Either's partner
19. Blurred and/or reddened
21. One time
23. WL claimed their child was a female with smallpox & prayed for its ___.
24. Mooed
25. Multi-story Buddhist tower
26. Small two-wheeled carriage pulled by 1 or 2 people
29. Robber
31. Passionate; full of strong feeling or enthusiasm
33. To make dry or thirsty
34. Wang Lung died these red and gave them to friends to celebrate the birth of his son.
35. Passively agreeable
39. WL's father would not do this
40. Ate
41. She married Wang Lung
43. Highest point
44. Wand Lung's first mistress

DOWN

1. To escape the soldiers, WL --- during the day
2. Reprimand; scold
3. 'He lived in the rich city as alien as a ___ in a rich man's house.'
4. A raised platform
5. Position of superiority
7. Difficult
8. Working on it made WL well again
9. Objected
11. Having or showing great wealth
16. Thrifty; tight with money
20. Lack of energy; listlessness
22. Cringing in fear
24. Reluctant
26. Harvested; cut and collected
27. Ill-humored
28. Unreasonably ill-tempered
30. Refrain from eating
31. In a state of wonder or amazement
32. Definite article
33. Deserving pity
36. Gruff
37. A kind of gem stone
38. O-lan bound her daughter's ___
42. Negative reply

VOCABULARY CROSSWORD ANSWER KEY - *The Good Earth*

VOCABULARY WORKSHEET 1 - *The Good Earth*

____ 1. Having or showing great wealth
    A. Opulent   B. Dallied   C. Dais   D. Reaped

____ 2. Ill-humored
    A. Incessant   B. Berate   C. Contrived   D. Shrewish

____ 3. Unreasonably ill-tempered
    A. Volubly   B. Purged   C. Petulant   D. Eminence

____ 4. Multi-story Buddhist tower
    A. Volubly   B. Zenith   C. Eminence   D. Pagoda

____ 5. Quiet; still; inactive
    A. Clad   B. Quiescent   C. Zenith   D. Concubines

____ 6. Gruff
    A. Wizened   B. Surly   C. Languor   D. Consternation

____ 7. Mooed
    A. Malice   B. Demurred   C. Lowed   D. Clad

____ 8. Contortion
    A. Dallied   B. Ricksha   C. Concubines   D. Writhe

____ 9. To be discontented or in low spirits
    A. Repine   B. Malice   C. Coquetry   D. Musing

____ 10. Continuous
    A. Loath   B. Berate   C. Incessant   D. Distraught

____ 11. Conscientious; exact
    A. Petulant   B. Scrupulous   C. Piteous   D. Agape

____ 12. Flirting
    A. Unctuous   B. Clad   C. Coquetry   D. Shrewish

____ 13. Lack of energy; listlessness
    A. Languor   B. Wizened   C. Peevish   D. Coquetry

____ 14. Objected
    A. Repine   B. Demurred   C. Peevishly   D. Clad

____ 15. Emotionally upset
    A. Dais   B. Obeisance   C. Quiescent   D. Distraught

____ 16. Slick; also characterized by insincere earnestness
    A. Volubly   B. Unctuous   C. Lowed   D. Concubines

____ 17. Characterized by fluent speech
    A. Volubly   B. Distraught   C. Cowering   D. Shrewish

____ 18. Ate
    A. Malice   B. Virtuously   C. Supped   D. Scrupulous

____ 19. Like a slave
    A. Compelled   B. Unctuous   C. Boisterously   D. Slavishly

____ 20. Gestures of homage, deference or reverence
    A. Virtuously   B. Clad   C. Consternation   D. Obeisance

VOCABULARY WORKSHEET 2 - *The Good Earth*

____ 1. RICKSHA A. Passionate; full of strong feeling or enthusiasm

____ 2. BLEARY B. To be discontented or in low spirits

____ 3. PEEVISHLY C. Withered; wrinkled

____ 4. WIZENED D. A raised platform

____ 5. DAIS E. Considering thoughtfully

____ 6. ARDUOUS F. To long for; to have feelings of tenderness for

____ 7. REPINE G. Quiet; still; inactive

____ 8. QUIESCENT H. Slick; also characterized by insincere earnestness

____ 9. CONTRIVED I. Making less of something

____ 10. INCESSANT J. In a contrary way; querulously

____ 11. LOATH K. Blurred and/or reddened

____ 12. ARDENT L. Mooed

____ 13. DEMURRED M. Objected

____ 14. YEARN N. Small two-wheeled carriage pulled by 1 or 2 people

____ 15. CONSTERNATION O. Difficult

____ 16. MALICE P. Continuous

____ 17. MUSING Q. A state of paralyzing dismay

____ 18. UNCTUOUS R. Intent of ill-will

____ 19. DEPRECIATION S. Reluctant

____ 20. LOWED T. Devised; planned; managed

KEY: VOCABULARY WORKSHEETS - *The Good Earth*

Worksheet 1	Worksheet 2
1. A	1. N
2. D	2. K
3. C	3. J
4. D	4. C
5. B	5. D
6. B	6. O
7. C	7. B
8. D	8. G
9. A	9. T
10. C	10. P
11. B	11. S
12. C	12. A
13. A	13. M
14. B	14. F
15. D	15. Q
16. B	16. R
17. A	17. E
18. C	18. H
19. D	19. I
20. D	20. L

VOCABULARY JUGGLE LETTER REVIEW GAME CLUES - *The Good Earth*

SCRAMBLED	WORD	CLUE
ECQATISCEUN	ACQUIESCENT	Passively agreeable
PAEGA	AGAPE	In a state of wonder or amazement
NRDTAE	ARDENT	Passionate; full of strong feeling or enthusiasm
USRUDOA	ARDUOUS	Difficult
RDEBEDGGE	BEGRUDGED	Gave reluctantly or resentfully
TERBEA	BERATE	Reprimand; scold
YLERAB	BLEARY	Blurred and/or reddened
OYOBTRSUSIEL	BOISTEROUSLY	Loudly; without restraint
ALCD	CLAD	Clothed
LOMLEEPDC	COMPELLED	Forced
BESNOCNCIU	CONCUBINES	Women contracted as second wives
NOONRETTAINSC	CONSTERNATION	A state of paralyzing dismay
VICDTRNOE	CONTRIVED	Devised; planned; managed
YQTUECOR	COQUETRY	Flirting
WIGRONCE	COWERING	Cringing in fear
SAID	DAIS	A raised platform
DELLAID	DALLIED	Tarried; loitered; also means flirted
REEDRUMD	DEMURRED	Objected
OTEPNIRCIDEA	DEPRECIATION	Making less of something
TIRAGUSTHD	DISTRAUGHT	Emotionally upset
NINEEEC	EMINENCE	Position of superiority
GRULAF	FRUGAL	Thrifty; tight with money
LEID	IDLE	Inactive; not working; being lazy
BEMBUTLIPRARE	IMPERTURBABLE	Unshakable; calm and steady
ROUNTIMGINP	IMPORTUNING	Persistently pleading
NUTDIMEP	IMPUDENT	Bold and offensive
SINANTSEC	INCESSANT	Continuous
GORNULA	LANGUOR	Lack of energy; listlessness
TALOH	LOATH	Reluctant
DEWOL	LOWED	Mooed
ELMAIC	MALICE	Intent of ill-will
NUMGIS	MUSING	Considering thoughtfully
ENBOSSIACE	OBEISANCES	Gestures of homage, deference or reverence
TOPLUNE	OPULENT	Having or showing great wealth
DAPOAG	PAGODA	Multi-story Buddhist tower
SHIPYVEEL	PEEVISHLY	In a contrary way; querulously
NETTLAPU	PETULANT	Unreasonably ill-tempered
SOTUPIE	PITEOUS	Deserving pity

Good Earth Vocabulary Clues Continued

PERDUG	PURGED	Purified; rid of undesirable elements
URYLLOQEUU	QUERULOUSLY	Grumblingly; complainingly
TISNUQCEE	QUIESCENT	Quiet; still; inactive
PAREED	REAPED	Harvested; cut and collected
MEERSOR	REMORSE	Bitter regret
INPEER	REPINE	To be discontented or in low spirits
KIRAHCS	RICKSHA	Small two-wheeled carriage pulled by 1 or 2 people
STUBOR	ROBUST	Full of strength and energy
LUUUSSPRCO	SCRUPULOUS	Conscientious; exact
WHERHISS	SHREWISH	Ill-humored
VASSHYLIL	SLAVISHLY	Like a slave
DUPPES	SUPPED	Ate
LUSRY	SURLY	Gruff
UNOSTUCU	UNCTUOUS	Slick; also characterized by insincere earnestness
TULVYROSUI	VIRTUOUSLY	Showing moral excellence, virtue or chastity
BOYLLVU	VOLUBLY	Characterized by fluent speech
ZINDEEW	WIZENED	Withered; wrinkled
TREWHI	WRITHE	Contortion
NEARY	YEARN	To long for; to have feelings of tenderness for
HEZTIN	ZENITH	Highest point

www.ingramcontent.com/pod-product-compliance
Lightning Source LLC
Chambersburg PA
CBHW051413070526
44584CB00023B/3407